THE
CREATIVE
MUSICIAN

IN THE CHURCH

by

KENT E. SCHNEIDER

Published by

THE CENTER FOR CONTEMPORARY CELEBRATION

West Lafayette, Indiana

Photography credits:

    Sr. Adelaide Ortegel, S.P., cover, 1,3,50,68,92,96,117,
                                     138,143,147
    Lorrayne Hockman, 23,63,165,172
    Sr. Cathy Campbell, S.P., 112,123
    Rev. Max Hale, 71
    Gary DeSmet, 87
    Rev. Richard Woods, O.P., 34-35
    Robert Wells, 191

Graphic design:

    Sr. Adelaide Ortegel, S.P.

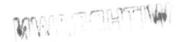

Table of Contents

*

PART FIVE

PART SIX

This book is dedicated to my grandfather who paid me
twenty-five cents a day if I would practice my trumpet
in the garage rather than in the house.

PART ONE

COMMUNICATING MUSICALLY

MUSIC IS WHAT YOU ARE

> You are a reflection of your music. Your whole life is
> so intertwined with your music that you don't know where
> one starts and where the other one ends. I'm not saying
> that music is everything in my life, but it is certainly
> a great part of my life.
>
> John "Dizzy" Gillespie, trumpeter

This day you have received the world around you, taking in data and information, feelings and ideas and you are in the process of making that world-as-it-
is-going-on have meaning for you. Then you give back to the world the fresh
interpretation of life, which is uniquely yours to give. You endow creation
with yourself. You are that freedom, you take the expressive risk.

The abilities to sense the world and to create sound or gesture are basic for
our becoming human. We communicate with our whole body. We dance, sing, shout,
mime, play instruments, tell stories (and later develop religions) in order to
get out what's inside us. As we move wholly through the world, we are able to
sense our particular presence as we communicate to others and they communicate
with us. We are always in dialogue. We cannot live a monologue life.

Every human being, no matter how young or old, is an urge to communicate. This,
I believe, is the distinguishing characteristic of our life-long journey in becoming human persons.

   We need to communicate what is inside in order to exist.

> *Blues is B.B. King. Yes, and I've been a crusader for it*
> *for years. Without this, I don't think I could live very*
> *long — not that I think I'm going to live a long time any-*
> *way, but I don't think I could live even that long if I had*
> *to stop playin' or if I couldn't be with people I love so,*
> *the people that have helped me so much...... I couldn't live!*

> The Sound of Soul (Chicago: Henry Regnery Co.,1969)
> by Phyl Garland, p. 104

Our personal interior needs to be outered in order to make that basic life
statement: "I am somebody!" Without this urge we would pass through life as
victims of an insensitive society:

   "You have eyes, but you cannot see. You have ears, but you cannot hear."

For me, the musician is a most powerful articulator of the world. As a
communicator, the creative musician tells about the way things are, and in the
process often reveals as much about how life is within himself as he does in
enabling us to perceive life within ourselves.

Music is a self-revealing language. It is impossible to hide your Self, musically speaking. Because of this quality of revelation, creative music and the creative musician have particularly important roles in the communication of God's Spirit in the world.

Music is your own experience, your thoughts, your wisdom.
If you don't live it, it won't come out of your horn.

Charlie Parker, saxophonist

from <u>Black Talk</u> (New York: Holt, Rinehart
& Winston, 1971) p. 18 by Ben Sidran

A UNIVERSAL LANGUAGE

How is it that we can speak of music as a "universal language"?

To say that anything is "universal" is an obvious exaggeration. Even in music a person hears what he wants to hear and chooses to integrate the experience in terms of personal needs. Yet it is true that music is able to communicate an idea, and convey an emotion without having to be translated into a particular dialect. Music is beyond translation in words because it is a language of feeling.

A key reason why music goes beyond words is that it is made up of basic elements common to all human experience: a sense of rhythm and a sense of tonal dynamic.

Rev. Schneider, Ira Sullivan and choirs rehearse in Miami, Florida
for a concert of religious jazz (1975).

RHYTHM IS THE PULSE OF LIFE

If it sounds good and got that beat, that's all you need. You don't
have to wonder what it is, it's got to be music. And it all comes from
the sanctified churches. How you gonna get away from it? That's where
the beat started. Those sisters get to shouting and boy, the church
would be rolling.

Louis Armstrong

Rhythm is the sensing of the world's aliveness. It is the expression of the
inner moving of God, man and the world. Under the microscope, the macrocosm
of rhythmic life is revealed in its complexity. Through the telescope, the
earth is seen in rhythmic relationship to the other planets. The seasons and
oceans, the subtle shifts of the continents, are all signs of this cyclical
rhythmic change. Our environment is alive with rhythm.

We are also alive with a pulse of life. From that first moment of birth, as we
emerge from the womb into the world, we begin our rhythm in life with a breathing in and a breathing out. Not only will we breath in rhythm, we will soon
learn to talk, run, write, paint with "rhythmic strokes" and make melodies
that are filled with rhythm. We have no option when it comes to getting involved with rhythm. It is impossible to merely observe the pulse of life.
Our built-in sense of timing is really an extension of our heart beat, which
pulses at 72 beats per minute, and our cerebral hemispheres, which are in
perpetual swing, day and night. We know that bodily exercise will increase the
heart rate. We shall learn that music which is played rapidly will also tend
to increase our pulse. Medical science shows that the slightest change in
body motion, even the opening and closing of the eyes, will cause change in the
brain rhythm and our emotions. Music also can effect our emotional rhythm.

It seems strange that so many people fear rhythm in music,
particularly when "music with a beat" is used in the church.
When we live in such a rhythmic world and affirm that God is
creator of the universe, it is a contradiction to deny something which is so natural to our existence, namely rhythm, a
place in the music which praises the One who set the world
in motion.

Some people condemn the use of "music with a beat" because
they feel it is too emotional to be spiritual. But I have
never known anyone who I regarded as a "spiritual person" who
wasn't also an emotional person. I don't think you can
separate being spiritual from being real, and authentic.

Dave Brubeck once pointed out that we're all fellow travelers
on the earth and we've all got a heart. That heart beat has
a certain beat for all people. This heart beat rhythm may be
the one beat that binds us all together. How can we deny
rhythm of the heart in music that is to speak to the soul?

Primitive man's awareness of this basic rhythm led to attempts at imitating and re-creating the rhythms of nature. The mystery that pulses in the world awakens the rhythmic intuition of mankind and the desire to discover the forces within the environment.

> "There is a sound which is fraught with mystery, a sound which is nature's magic, for by it dumb things can speak. When that strange and curious man first struck together two pieces of wood, he had other aims than his own delight in sensuous sound, he was trying to re-create something that had bewildered him. That something was rhythmic sound — on which roots the art of music."

> from <u>The Dancing Chimpanzee</u>, Leonard Williams

At first, mankind was in awe of the sounds of life's rhythm. Then, as we all listened more carefully, we began to sense the pulse and we began to imitate what we heard. We began to create and re-state, in new ways, what we were hearing. We began to organize our sense of time into beats of metered pattern. In the process of moving from a feeling of awe to a feeling of mastering the sounds of life we lost the sense of mystery that is within the world. We took life's pulse and made it into time and metered patterns, until today, most of our sense of rhythm is more of a synchronization of the culture.

Synchronization is not bad. It is functional, enabling a large group of people to work as a single unit. Synchronization accomplishes a great deal.

> Synchronized timing takes a group of students and shapes them into a marching band. It makes armies move by standardizing their mobility. It makes football teams work with precision, hence the often applied term "machine." A rowing team will pull "as one" with synchronized efforts.

> Synchronization is also part of the "timing" of mass-produced culture. It takes people and fits them into a pattern (or meter) in order to produce materials and consumer goods more efficiently.

But what happens to the individual when he or she is synchronized? How much freedom can one exercise when a part of a synchronized movement? Usually, very little. Instead of using rhythm to "set ourselves free" we have used rhythm to keep things moving smoothly in an orderly fashion. We've lost the freedom of rhythm.

I have a hunch that a similar situation is present in the church. We do not sing the hymns with spirit, we sing them with synchronization. We do not play our instrument with spirit, we play with synchronization. Like I said before, synchronization allows a large group of people to function smoothly and orderly. No wonder people get up-tight when a group plays music in the church that allows for some personal "freedom of expression", such as in jazz music. The music is threatening the "orderliness" of the synchronized service. There is nothing sacred about being synchronized.

In a following chapter, I'll probe this area further. However, for now, let me summarize this section:

In the process of developing our ability to shape sound and make
rhythm, we've lost our sense of the mystery of life as we've become
dominated by a sense of time. Our most conspicuous use of time is
that which I call "synchronized time", which motivates people to
get to work on time, finish on time, move and play in time. We are
accountable for merely "killing time" or wasting the moments we have.
This sense of timing invariably carries over into our music rhythm
and the way in which we play and sing the music of the church. If
we are truly concerned about sharing music that is filled with Spirit
and life, then we must find the path that leads to regaining a sense
of rhythm without losing our sense of what time it is.

TONAL DYNAMICS: The Breath of Life

Then the Lord God formed Adam from dust and breathed
into his nostrils the breath of life: and he became
a living being.

from <u>Genesis</u>

Understanding the dynamics of tones and their power to communicate comes from
our own need to produce vocal sounds from our first moments of birth. From our
experiences in using vocal sounds we become sensitive to pitch differences:
when we raise the voice pitch, the intensity and sound becomes louder; when we
lower the pitch, the sound becomes softer. If we raise the voice from its
normal range of two or three adjoining tones, the pitch invariably hits a fifth
tone above the normal pitch, assuming that the normal pitch is the first tone of
a musical scale. When we are stirred by emotions, the voice will reach an octave.
It is highly possible that the first earthly inhabitants hollered and shouted
their octaves and fifths long before they tried to sing them.

Tones, like words, communicate a person's inner intensity. We understand the
movement of tones as they rise and fall in space partially because we have experienced the physical movement of our bodies through space. Physically, it
takes greater energy to leap, to raise ourselves up from a lying position, to
run fast or to jump. It requires less energy to relax, to lie down or to slide.
These familiar experiences fill out imagination so that when tones rise we sense
the increase in effort and when they fall we sense the relaxation in terms of
our own physical experience. Tones that simply "float," such as a sustained
tone of stringed instruments or the beautiful sound made by rubbing a wet
finger along the rim of a crystal glass, also "make the listener float" imagin-
atively.

<u>The Meaning of Tonal Dynamic</u>

What does one tone communicate?
In most cases it communicates very little. Perhaps a single tone might communicate a warning (sirens, air raid, bell toll) just as single words like "help"
or "fire" are warning signals.

Tone takes on meaning only as it enters into relationship to other tones. This
relation may be a linear one to form melodies, or it may be a horizontal one to

form harmonies, or it may be a series of linear waves of tones to form counterpoint.

> Today we're not used to hearing counterpoint because so much of the music is harmony...a melody on top with pillars of chords supporting it from beneath.
>
> In a world that is permeated by multi-layers of rhythm, we are singing church music from the 1800's that lacks counterpoint, both tonally and rhythmically. Our music is too often characteristic of the sense of a dramatic flow or a wave of tones that build and ebb. In our urgency to be "precise" musically, we've taken the spirit out of the tones we sing.
>
> In Bach's time, people listened to music differently. They heard lines of simultaneous melodies, rather than chords. Though this may seem strange to us, counterpoint preceeded harmony. Today we need to regain an ear for counterpoint.

It may be helpful for you to think of tones-in-relation as being like a wave of movement through time and space. The wave will rise and fall and will always keep moving as a thrust towards completing itself. The dynamic action of meaning that comes from tones interacting with each other is much like the way words interact to finish a sentence or a thought. Alone, a tone (word) may mean something, but when you place that tone (word) in relation to another, a new meaning comes about that is greater than either of the two tones. This is a transformation event, one that is filled with a sense of mystery. The music had consisted of single tones which now has been changed as the tones relate to each other in the total work. It is because of this transformation event, that we are able to understand the musical experience, for we don't listen to the parts, we listen to the whole.

TUNING IN TO THE MUSICAL EXPERIENCE

Have you ever known someone who was always trying to hold on to life and never really lived life at all? I have. In fact, I sometimes try to build "corrals" around loves and hopes, thinking that I will preserve the meaning of the experience if I can just keep those feelings around me. But, I soon learn that trying to hold on to life is like trying to box up running water. If you succeed in containing the moving water, you've dulled the very quality that first attracted you to it. Life-giving water, that is boxed up, will become stagnant and will not support life.

We must always be prepared to be moving and learning new thoughts, being open to the fullness of experiencing each new day. If we ever get to the point where we feel that we've mastered living, we'll find that we've only succeeded in boxing ourselves up, out of touch with life-giving experience.

> "What must I do to experience life?" said the rich man.
> And, Jesus told him: "You must give all that you have.
> Only as you lose your life, will you truly find it."

We must be open to "experience" and not closed off. So often we would like to fill those uncharted spaces in life with mere repetition of what has already been known. The truly open person knows that even those most carefully explored regions of life have not really been covered at all. There is always more to experience.

One reason why music can be such a source of inspirational experience is that it provides the hope that there is meaning even in the passingness of the moment.

> A tone does not exist forever. It says what it must say and then gives way for another tone to speak. With our memory we remember the gift of the one tone as another tone enters. In that relationship of tones comes the meaning of the musical experience. How we choose to put tones together is comparable in artistry to the work of the film-maker who edits frames of visual images, or the potter who pieces together sections of clay to transform them into a new wholeness.

Music also teaches us to live with expectations of the future.

> We learn to live with a trust even though we don't always know what's ahead in time or in the composers mind. The next note will be coming, although we may not know what it will sound like. In music, we gain experience in anticipating the future with interest instead of fear.

WHAT IS "MUSICAL EXPERIENCE"?

Any "experience," whether it's musical, religious, physical or spiritual, is a vitalization of the person. Through an experience, I sense myself and the world in a new way. Something is awakened in me that wasn't in my awareness before. It may be painful or quite joyous.

An "experience" is an event: It sets a precedent. It is usually not a repeatable commodity in that you will never get the same "experience" in the same way twice. Experiences are difficult to re-tell in their fullness. You simply have to be present to have shared the "experience."

> It's reported that a person came up to Louis Armstrong and asked him to describe what is 'jazz' music. Armstrong responded by saying that "if you don't know what it is, then you haven't heard it." What he was saying was that if you've experienced jazz and its style of freedom and spontaneity, then you wouldn't need to ask someone to tell you about it. There are certain events you have to feel first-hand.

Without feelings, there can be no experience. We exist only to the degree that we are a caring, feeling people. By 'feeling' I do not mean simply glandular emotion, programmed sensations, shock treatment or acting on the impulse. Feeling is tuning into the pulse of life and sharing the breath of life with another. Feeling is sensing with my whole self and drawing upon the wealth of previous feelings around which I organize my life.

> One of my most vivid musical experiences was in listening to a premiere performance of Murray Schaeffer's "Threnody" composed for orchestra, choir, electronic tape and speaking voices. The sound took me out of the auditorium and gave me the sensation of being part of the crew

flying the bomber over Hiroshima. Suddenly I was on the ground with a collage of burning houses and humans when the bomb hit. I heard the reported account of a small girl who had just been playing with some friends in front of her home and how everything was blown away. The skin on her hands hung from her finger tips like a glove turned inside-out. The music sounded the horror.

Though the sound was combined with words and readings, screams and howls, I was caught up in the whole meaning of the work. I ceased to be concerned with the details that laid the foundation for my understanding. I experienced the "point" of the whole sounding. Even when the medium of communication was verbal, my point of consciousness was no longer of verbalisms. It was a perception of a full reality of experience — an awareness in which every sensuous, intellectual, and emotional perception focused to a point.

The musical experience will not only be emotional, it will also spark thoughts; perhaps affirming the love God has for mankind, the need for human dignity with all people, the awareness of injustice in the world. It may even cause me to act upon what I believe. The musical experience brings me into the awareness of reality and the truth or falsity of the 'sound proposition' presented to the listener. Music can sound vivid truth.

The musical experience is an integration of inner imagery of the mind and feelings and the outer sensing of the music itself which takes form in time and space. The musical experience will mean different things to different people. It will have various degrees of vividness because sounds will stir a variety of inner images and thoughts within each person. Though the "outer sound" may be heard in the same way, the inner integration of the music with a person's previous experience will vary.

When a woman heard the first performance of Bach's "St. Matthew's Passion," she remarked: "'Tis surely a musical comedy." That just goes to prove that one man's Bach is another man's Babel.

The musical experience is certainly dependent upon its cultural context. Just as a foreign language will have little meaning to people who do not speak it, so sound will have little meaning to people who do not understand it. The musical concept must be accessible to the communal culture, if it is to have meaning. Fortunately, in today's world, music is beginning to overflow the boundaries of one country and is now available to the entire world through the media of recordings and radio. Barriers that once prevented certain styles of music from being played in the church are gradually coming down simply because the music of today is expanding our culture.

I remember in 1966, when the Dukes of Kent and I started playing jazz in churches, how up-tight some of the people would be with the thought of a "jazz band" in the sanctuary. That conditioning was the result of their growing up at a time in history when "jazz music" was locked in the speakeasy and bars. For some people the style of music and the musicians were unfamiliar. What motivates these musicians to play this kind of music for the praise of God?

We've gone through a period of exploration and liturgical searchings. Religious songs have been influencing the pop charts (Amazing Grace, Morning Has Broken, etc.) and the folk, rock and jazz idioms have been influencing the church. I think this kind of integration is a healthy sign. No longer will we have "sacred verses secular." We will simply have music that is good and appropriate and music that is terribly inappropriate.

Musical experience opens us up to the new and sometimes the unknown. It may even challenge my personal pattern of the way I organize my life. This kind of change for the routine or taken-for-granted style of living (or music) causes people to think and to evaluate the meaning of what they are doing in light of a new discovery.

As I hear it, the church is in need of a new sound revolution. We must break away from the stereotypical response patterns which a musical culture of another era has dictated. We should not limit the interchange of ideas, musical experiences or the creative introduction of new styles of music to what is "safe and sure." The Christian faith teaches us to build upon a foundation which has been growing since the early church gathered. But we must keep building for the growth of the People of God is not complete.

We are in constant need of the new hymns and new songs which affirm the Christian life for today. It will not be enough to sing of a faith that was expressed two hundred or two thousand years ago without investing some of our own faith-making statements in those songs.

> Bring on the hymns that speak of Christ-alive in today's world!
>
> Sing out new melodies that give credence to our words!
>
> Sound the trumpets and saxes, the drums and guitars, the flutes and electric pianos. Let everything that breathes praise God!
>
> Play the notes of whatever your musical expression of thanksgiving may be. Don't get caught with your instrument in its case, or your electricity unplugged, or with your strings unstrung when the call comes. Whatever you do, play the notes the very best you can!

Further Reading

THE EFFECTS OF MUSIC, Max Schoen.   New York: Harcourt,
    Brace and Company, Inc., 1927.

EMOTIONS AND MEANING IN MUSIC, Leonard B. Meyer.   Chicago:
    The University of Chicago Press, 1956.

A HISTORY OF MUSICAL THOUGHT, Donald N. Ferguson.   Minne-
    apolis: University of Minnesota Press, 1960.

THE MUSICAL EXPERIENCE OF COMPOSER, PERFORMER, LISTENER,
    Roger Sessions.   Princeton, New Jersey: Princeton
    University Press, 1971.

MUSIC AND IMAGINATION, Aaron Copeland.   New York: Mentor
    Books, 1952.

MUSIC AND YOUR MIND — Listening with a New Consciousness,
    Helen L. Bonny and Louis M. Savary.   New York: Collins
    Associates Publishing, Inc., 1973.

THE RATIONAL AND SOCIAL FOUNDATIONS OF MUSIC, Max Weber.
    Carbondale: Southern Illinois University Press, 1958.

SOUND AND SYMBOL: MUSIC AND THE EXTERNAL WORLD, Victor
    Zuckerkandl.   New York: Pantheon Books, 1956.

GIVING MUSIC PERSONAL FORM

> The truth consists not in <u>knowing</u> the truth, but in
> <u>being</u> the truth.
>
> Søren Kierkegaard, theologian

We are always in danger of simply going through life having memorized
certain patterns that seem to work in many situations. We parrot
back definitions that get us through school. Our society values a
person by what that person knows rather than by what he or she is.
But knowing how to live is not really living. The only way we can
live is by actually doing it. To know how to love is not loving.
We must actually reach out and love someone. It is not enough to
simply know the Christian faith. We must live it out.

It is the same way with the musician: it is not enough that we "know
the notes." <u>We must be the music.</u>

> "We are the music we play. And our commitment is to
> peace, to understanding of life. And we keep trying
> to purify our music, to purify ourselves, so that we
> can move ourselves - and those who hear us - to higher
> levels of peace and understanding. I'm convinced that
> through music life can be given more meaning.
>
> "I'm trying to communicate to as many people as I can.
> It's late now for the world. And if I can help raise
> people to new plateaus of peace and understanding, I'll
> feel my life has been worth living as a spiritual
> artist's; that's what counts."
>
> Albert Ayler, saxophonist

The musician must strive to reach a level where he or she doesn't have
to worry about "making the notes." The techniques of the instrument
get mastered and become tools for expression. We need to rise to a
stage where we will feel able to invest ourselves into the music we
play. In other words, we are able to give music per-sonal forming
whenever we perform.

How does the word "performer" hit you? Does it leave you with negative
or positive feelings? Do you ever think of yourself as a performer in
church, one who gives per-sonal form to the music?

In a recent workshop, I asked the participants what the word "performer" meant for them. The responses ranged from a "show-off,"
an "entertainer," to a "gifted person with talent" and a "person
who can interpret something well."

I believe that it is good to become a "per-sonal former" of music in the church. By this I mean that the person risks something of himself or herself in shaping the music before us. The person pours out some of the self in interpreting the feelings of the music. Without this kind of investing of a personal style, the music becomes a repeatable commodity; something we could hear in that way at any time. The listeners become dull to the sound because they no longer listen with an expectancy that something might happen. The music has a "cut and dried" quality.

The creative musician is always putting himself into the music. There is no other way to go about it. In this style of per-sonal forming, the player seeks to go beyond himself and to reach new depths of expressiveness. In the church, the per-former becomes one with the congregation, inviting them to also go beyond themselves in response to his calling. But the musical communication does not stop with the per-former. The musician becomes a transparency, like a window that opens to the Spirit, letting God work through the sound and feeling of the person.

John Coltrane wrote the following letter to those who listen to his album A LOVE SUPREME:

Dear Listener:

All Praise Be To God To Whom All Praise Is Due.

During the year 1957, I experienced, by the grace of God, a spiritual awakening which was to lead me to a richer, fuller, more productive life. At that time, in gratitude, I humbly asked to be given the means and privilege to make others happy through music. I feel this has been granted through His grace. ALL PRAISE TO GOD.

As time and events moved on, a period of irresolution did prevail. I entered into a phase which was contradictory to the pledge and away from the esteemed path; but thankfully, now and again through the unerring and merciful hand of God, I do perceive and have been duly re-informed of His Omnipotence, and of our need for, and dependence on Him. At this time I would like to tell you that No Matter What...It Is With God. He Is Gracious And Merciful. His Way Is Through Love, In Which We All Are. It Is Truly—A Love Supreme—.

This album is a humble offering to Him. An attempt to say "THANK YOU GOD" through our work, even as we do in our hearts and with our tongues. May He help and strengthen all men in every good endeavor.

The per-sonal former of music fills the sound with an enthusiasm (meaning to be filled with God) and brings an attitude of freshness to the playing, as if he were <u>discovering the art all over again</u>. That's not easy to do every time you pick up your instrument. It required an endurance and a love of what you are doing to communicate all that is inside.

MUSICALLY SPEAKING

Do you remember how you first learned to talk?

> First you listened to what others were saying. Then, with encouragement, you began imitating and repeating what people said to you. Perhaps you explored other sounds that sounded like nonsense. You learned a few words and began using them in sentences. You started reading books. You began inventing your own sentences to say what was inside of you. You developed your inflections, tones in your voice that made your way of speaking different from anyone else's.

Your speaking identifies you as a unique person in all the world. What you say and the way you say it is your style.

Learning to speak in a musical language is much the same process. Think for a moment how you learned to make music.

> You probably listened to music on the radio or on a record. With family encouragement, you got your first horn and a teacher who taught you to read the notes and to make the fingerings. The teacher played for you, and you, perhaps, tried to imitate what you saw and heard. Your first sounds might have been terrible, but, with practice, you began to play scales, melodic phrases and songs. You went on to read from more advanced music books. You learned to play the "classic" solos and compositions for your instrument.

> You have acquired all this technique of the instrument and now you could go on to creating your own ideas, melodic phrases and songs. You could develop your own style of inflections and characteristic tone of the instrument that makes your way of playing different from that of anyone else's.

At what stages, in speaking verbally as well as musically, do you create, give per-sonal forming to your own feelings and ideas?

Many church musicians have not yet moved from the stage of

IMITATION - where I try to sound like someone else

to

INTERPRETATION - where I try to put myself into the sound.

I was conducting a workshop with a church in a Chicago
suburb and had the privilege of working with the principal
cellist from the symphony. We were doing a session on
Scripture and the use of solo instruments for interpreting
the meaning of the words. I asked the woman to interpret
Psalm 8, which asks: "What is man that God is mindful of
him?" She said: "Do you have the music? I can't play
anything without the music." Here was a person with a
great skill at playing what was printed, but had never
ventured out to play what she felt inside.

We worked for about half an hour reading through the Psalm,
asking each other what feelings certain words had, and
then trying to put those feelings into tones.

When we shared the Psalm with the community, I read it
while she played. The woman was nervous, but in control
of herself. As we got more and more into the reading, she
forgot herself and became one with the instrument. As we
finished, some of the congregation was crying - the words
had taken on new meaning with the cello sound and had
touched deeply inside us all.

The woman often writes to tell me how she is still
working at her improvising.

Speaking at a conference on Church Music, Dave Brubeck, jazz pianist
and composer, told about his childhood days of learning the piano:

"I remember violin bows coming at me when I'd make a
mistake. The whole idea of reading music was "better
duck if you miss a note." I was using my ear more than
I was using my eyes. I had the great quality of staring
at the music as if I were reading it and coming pretty
close to the right notes and people didn't realize that
I couldn't read. Then, when I got to college, it became
embarrassing to tell people that I couldn't read. So
I started a whole process of avoiding it in order to
not ruin my family name."

Music is not a language of the eye, but of the ear. It is meant to
be heard rather than read. The same situation applies to the minister's
sermon. It is meant to be <u>heard</u>, not read. How do most of us "learn
music"? By reading it, don't we? If we continue to learn "how to read"
music and never take time to play what we hear inside, we will not develop the ability to communicate at an interpretive level.

IMITATION OR INTERPRETATION

The essential distinction between the musician who imitates and the
musician who interprets is the difference of sounding like someone else
or sounding like yourself.

The Imitator

The imitator may be a fine technician who can sound just like the
greatest player. However, if music is a personal form of speech,
then music which is simply imitative is lacking in a personal quality.
Too much of church music is of this impersonal nature. Imitative
music is usually safe to present in church because it involves no
personal risk on the part of the player or choir. If someone doesn't
like the music, you can always shrug it off and say, "Well, that was
somebody else's work. That wasn't really me, anyway." Most of the
imitative music of the church is played by someone who is still at
the stage of "reading music." The visual literacy of a musician
dominates the church as it does our whole society.

What did musicians do before music could be printed in mass quantities?
The musician was expected to create some of the music that would be
used in the church of his region. Have we lost that art?

Prior to the sixteenth century, music was often defined by the place
where it was played. A song sung in a saloon was a "tavern song"; one
that accompanied drinking would be a "drinking song"; one that was
used in the church would be a "church song." There was nothing in-
herent in the music that would allow the people to define the music
as "churchy" or "secular." There was, as there is today, only good
and bad music. Perhaps this situation accounts for the practice of
borrowing melodies from the saloons for use with church hymns, as
did Luther and Bach.

It wasn't until music began to be printed that we had the distinction
between the composer and the performer. The printed page made every
musician an interpreter of the composer's idea. Instead of hearing
the composer interpret his own work, we received the musical notation
in a second-hand way. The musician could read it rather than hear
it. With music becoming more and more available, the need for self-
expression was diminished. No longer did the church musician need to
be an originator.

The Interpreter

The interpreter is a musician who goes outside himself to dwell in another's work or reveals himself in the improvised creation of what is felt inside.

To interpret another's work is to make the Spirit of the composer be present to the listener. It is a kind of resurrection event. This is how I feel about the artistry of Virgil Fox whose drive in life is to perform the music of Bach so that the people on the street can understand the composer. Fox tries to remain true to the spirit of Bach and interprets that spirit as if Bach were alive today using a specially-designed electronic organ and a multi-media light team. While the "purists" argue that Fox is not using the same kind of instrument that Bach used and, therefore, does not sound like Bach, the role of the interpreter is not to sound like or imitate, but to re-create the music in a per-sonal forming. We don't need to worry about having to make good music "contemporary." Good music is always "contemporary."

> The theologian, Kierkegaard, wrote that people do not need to worry about making Christ contemporary, for He is always contemporary with us... not even two thousand years can change what He is.
>
> It is the same with the interpreter, for he must remain true to the spirit of the work he seeks to make real. In the very act of interpreting, he is putting himself into the work. If the musician does not, then he is simply keeping a safe distance from real communication. To anything we interpret, we must give per-sonal form or else we are simply facsimiles.

One of the most authentic interpreters I know of is Ira Sullivan, a devoted musician and a man of faith who has been doing a lot of playing in churches since 1967. In an interview in DOWNBEAT magazine, February 17, 1974, he talks about how he works with musicians to open themselves up to creating music:

> "I try to get the musicians to the point where they can enjoy varied musical experiences if they open themselves up to various expressions. How does one get across that we should become consummate artists in anything we do? I believe that the only way one can accomplish this is to be happy and at least try to fulfill oneself.
>
> "Some musicians seem to think: 'God forbid that I should listen to you and learn something; then it wouldn't be all me inside.' Many musicians believe that John Coltrane, Ornette Coleman, Charlie Parker and the Beatles just sprung,

as it were, full blown from the sow's ear, playing like masters. They think all you have to do is to learn a few of the hit records and you are going to be a master."

Ira said that he felt his musical situation was best when he was playing the instrument and not thinking about notes or changes. "I have a corner on this market since I know notes, but I do not know changes, so I don't think academically about music. I feel that I'm at my best when I can free myself completely from the effort of trying to put something out and feel more like I am the instrument being played— like opening the channel to God or whatever it is. I suddenly get the feeling that I'm standing next to myself, listening to another musician. I am listening to myself, but I'm not thinking that this is me playing. It's just that one gets so inside oneself that total communication takes over.

"One opens up. The physical problem of making the music — pressing the valves down and using the muscles in your mouth, etc. — all of this goes out the window. I never think of these things. Now, if one can do this without becoming cognizant of it, without getting scared or considering how good it feels, as one does when initially experiencing this, the musician is in good form. The minute he questions himself on how he is doing this, the experience is over."

The creating experience, where you and your instrument are one and the ideas flow from you as you hear them inside, is an exhilarating and very delicate moment. In the next chapter on The Meaning of Being Creative, we will explore the dimension of the creative action as interpreted in scripture and by some musicians who have lived in the midst of that action.

THE MEANING OF "BEING CREATIVE"

> At the beginning God expressed himself. That personal expression, that word, was with God and was God, and he existed with God from the beginning. All creation took place through him and none took place without him. In him appeared life and this life was the light of mankind. The light still shines in the darkness, and the darkness has never put it out.
>
> John 1:1 Phillips Translation

In the beginning God communicated. He made his Presence known to mankind in the person of Jesus Christ. God became understandable to a world that knew itself in physical and material ways. The Word of God, God's Sound, became incarnate and lived with us in a particular historical embodiment called Jesus of Nazareth. It was through this realization of God's Presence in Jesus that there was a uniquely powerful symbol of the divine. The Christ is the transparent symbol pointing beyond himself to the divine Center of Creation through which everything has life energy. Jesus Christ is the extension of God in action in the world. In Christ is the fidelity and the truth of the One who created Him. The Creator and the Creation, while two distinct beings, yet share a commonality that is their oneness. "I am one with the Father," said Jesus. The incarnation is fulfilled when the Creator becomes identified with that which he creates. God is one with the Christ. It is the same with creative people: a musician is recognized by his or her music, a painter by his painting style; and the inner movings of a Picasso create the outer sculptured forms of what Picasso is.

There are two dimensions to the creative act:

> first, there is the inner act which forms within the Creator. This is the power of imagination in which the creation is seen in its fullness. This is an inner act and is timeless;

> secondly, there is the outer act which is the realization or incarnation of the imaginative idea. What was in the mind is now set in the world. What was once timeless is now set into time. What was once spirit is now given material form subject to all the limitations of a material world. What was once imperishable now is open to distortion, even to destruction.

Everyone is able to share in the first stage of the creative action because every person is imaginative. However, not everyone shares in the second stage because not everyone is evolved enough to be able to express an idea in a way that other people will understand. This gift of expressing is the creative struggle and suffering that often goes on within an artist to break through the limitations of the world's materiality and bring an idea into fullness.

THE IMAGINATIVE IDEA

Each person is filled with imagination, an essential quality for the creative action.

Genesis says that God created us in his Image. We can interpret "Image" in a physical way, such as "you are the image of your Dad." But, as you look around at God's Creation, it becomes apparent that we don't all look alike. Being created in God's image must mean something other than looking alike.

I find meaning in interpreting this as being created in a Spiritual Image and likeness of God. God's Spirit Image is in everyone. We are an extension of God's Imagination. As I read the account, I feel that God creates us and fills us with his imagination which is the spiritual source for ideas.

Imagination is the ability to form mental images in the mind. A creator patterns the shape of what is to be arted. Decisions need to be made as to what form the expression will take in order to make the idea understandable. God can create out of nothingness, but we are not that kind of creators. It is our role to order the intelligible world, to give meaning, to be designers and fashioners, interpreters of life as it is experienced.

We need to nurture our imagination for if we let it lay dormant it will weaken like a muscle that is not used. Imagination, as I have experienced it, is more than dream-like trips into an escape world. It is the touching of a Spiritual source that keeps us alive and gives us alternatives to daily living. It is too easy to get boxed-up in life, to be entombed in mindless routines. Imagination is the spirit of "nevertheless" — when one way is blocked, our imagination opens other avenues of expressing ourselves in uniquely personal ways.

> The sounds made by a jazz musician are instantly identifiable as his own creation. Jazz is a personal form of speech. More than most other music, jazz reflects the personality of its creator. This relation between the personality of the jazz man and the distinctiveness of his music is one of the mysteries of musical creation and one of its

beauties. The personality of the man, the feel of a jazz style, these are expressions of spirit that resist being pinned down, but they can be seen and heard in action, and, like jazz itself, appreciated in the act of creation.

The idea is a gift. You don't really know what brings it about. You can be ready for it and you can have all the training that makes you able to produce it. The actual idea, the coming together of new forms, is a gift. Then you're responsible for bringing that gift into reality.

THE REALIZATION OF THE IDEA

We now must accompany the idea with an action, the desire to bring the idea into reality. To be filled with a creative readiness, the inner idea, is only part of the process. Many good ideas die off simply because we were never able to bring them into fullness.

For the musician, the realization of an idea is a calling-out. We ex-press ourselves, we actualize what is within, and create from our own substance.

But, the depth out of which we create will be different for each person as will our style of expression, given the musical techniques that we have to work with. The power of our communication often correlates with the depth out of which the idea rose.

> I think of a very lonely period in my life a few years ago and the only way I could express what I was feeling was musically. Words just couldn't say the feeling. It was one of my hardest struggles to find the sounds that would speak what was going on inside. Life was dark and the future not very bright. Loved ones had gone. I was questioning whether I really had anything to say musically— which is kind of like death.
>
> I began "composing" by playing my horn. I was searching for that combination of sounds that said where I was. Gradually the tones took form and I began stretching the melody into longer lines until it was completed. That process took about five hours to say what was inside. I did not write it down, though I did have a tape recorder running throughout the whole time. I didn't want to worry about stopping the flow of the ideas in order to notate what I was doing.

The next day I tried to remember the lines. (I have this thing about composing music — that, if it's good, I'll be able to remember it because the idea will still be living with me.) The melody came back with some new tones added that sounded even better to me.

I worked that day again much in the spirit of a painter who mixes and matches colors on canvas. Then, that night, I put the music on paper to "see" what I had been hearing for two days. Musically, the notes were searching, but with hope. Later, I wrote words to it for a friend. I titled it "Song of Love."

To realize an idea is a persistant struggle that goes on. Usually the realization falls short of the fullness of the original idea. Many creative people live their lives as a continual striving for the time when an idea can be fully heard, seen or felt.

Dave Brubeck is one artist that strives for the realization of the fullness of his ideas through improvisation:

"People say, 'Sit down and improvise, sit down and improvise. But, there are times, however, early in the morning when the work of God, or together with other musicians, or just playing by yourself, that something happens. This might be akin to 'religious experience.

"As an improviser, you activate the next move, the next split second. As a composer, you take your time. And, when you take your time, you hear it on paper. I prefer to work, if there is such a thing, again, with inspiration. I know that that is the way I work. Now, whether I am inspired or not is a question I ask myself. I think a composer has to adopt a motto: 'If you feel that flush on your cheeks, don't kid around. Get that pen going.'

"As a jazz musician, I know that truly great inspiration will come two or three times a year, when you're working every night. And, boy, when it comes, you will know that it's inspiration because you can't do anything wrong. You'll take chances that are physically impossible. I'm very religious about it. That's what can happen through inspiration, and it doesn't happen very often.

"I like to think of each snowfall being a different crystal. How many millions of snowflakes, each with a different pattern, must fall in one minute of snow. We cut ourselves off from inspiration all the time by putting up our own limits and by not realizing that everything is possible if you are in the right frame of mind with the right amount of experience in your art form or your way of communication.

"It's the same thing if you are giving a service from the pulpit and you've written it out. All of a sudden, you feel like leaving the text behind and really talking. From that moment, you begin to communicate because you are really saying something. The musician has a far greater opportunity to do this in church than the preacher."

The next chapter will explore the elements that are essential for genuine communication, particularly with the musician in the church.

In concert: Dolores Layer, Kent Schneider, Pat Burris and multimedia light company give jazz expression to a Bach fugue.

PERSONAL FORMING IS
GENUINE COMMUNICATION

Do you ever wonder why you are sometimes able to "make your point" better in certain situations than in others? Why do certain pieces of music seem to mean more to a congregation at different times?

In this section, we'll explore the elements of genuine communication:

The <u>WHO</u>   - what difference <u>you</u> make in communicating rather than someone else?

The <u>TO WHOM</u> - what do you know about the person or persons that you are communicating to, what are their needs, interests?

The <u>WHY</u>   - what is that inner motivation that makes you communicate?

The <u>HOW</u>   - what is your style?

The <u>WHERE</u> - the environment, the place is a framework for communication.

The <u>WHEN</u>   - the timeliness of what you are saying. Is it out-of-date?

WHO IS COMMUNICATING?

It really makes a difference who says something or plays something. The power of the communication is often determined by the stature of the person.

> For instance, when a chief speaks, in a tribal situation, his words carry much more weight than if a member of the tribe said the same words. However, once that chief's words become suspect, once his communication becomes un-true, his power to command attention is decreased simply because his believeability has been lost. There is a political cartoon of Richard Nixon speaking about how he will be vindicated once the truth of the Watergate Tapes comes out. In each successive cartoon, a little bit more of Nixon's body begins to disappear until finally there is just the image of his mouth saying, "Let me make this perfectly clear." On his suit was written the word "credibility."

The importance of what you say is connected with who you are.

> People will come to hear a composer perform his or her music because that person is able to witness to the music better than anyone else can. People come to hear music from its source of imagination, the creator. Or people may come to hear an interpreter of another's composition because that interpreter makes the music come alive. One gains a feeling that the interpreter has tuned into the spirit of the composer so well that the interpreter is the personal forming, the <u>per-former</u>, of the music before us.

Through the press, some musicians have gained great public reputations, but we must learn that you can't believe everything you read. I have sometimes come away disappointed after hearing a well-known performer playing material that was played the last time he came to town. Nothing new was communicated. There was little life present. In a sense, the musician had fallen back to a level of imitation — though he was imitating himself at a more creative moment. A person who repeats what has already been said is a person who retreats to the past where life has already been safely explored.

> *"Why worry about what's already created? Think about*
> *the beautiful of tomorrow. Think about what can better*
> *that which has already been created on this planet,*
> *giving good example for others. For you are the key to*
> *the world and the world will learn from you."*

> Pharaoh Sanders, saxophonist
> "The Beautiful of Tomorrow" album

How effectively others hear us is connected with the kind of integrity we are in the community. I'm always wary of the person who agrees to do everything and then, simply by the limitations of physical being, is able to accomplish very little. After a while, you take this person's words lightly. I'm also shy of the musician who gives verbal ascent to understanding what is needed but then can't deliver musically. We become known by our integrity.

Genuine communication is primarily a first-person experience. By this I mean, what we say or play is a witness to what we have lived through in a first-hand way. "I experienced this. I was there. I lived, suffered or rejoiced through it." I find sermons that are built upon quotes from others, or the latest books that the minister has read, to be rather second-hand. There is very little personal forming or risking of self in that kind of speaking. Sermons are not to be a lecture-review of books.

I also find that much of the music that is played in the churches today is of this second-hand quality. It is played like it is felt; removed from any kind of right-now feeling. If only a musician would take some time to help prepare the listeners for what they are about to hear by sharing some of the feeling the musician brings to the music, then the music might not seem so distant.

In a Thanksgiving Workshop in Lexington, Massachusetts, people composed songs around the idea of what it means to be "family." As part of the celebration, a woman and her two sons shared their feelings of family after the loss of the husband and father. Each member shared a personal statement. The youngest boy, about 9 years old, had written a song entitled "A Family Is Something Very Special." Before the service, he wasn't

sure whether he wanted to sing and play his guitar. But, if he
hadn't shared the music himself with the congregation, it would
have lost all the intensity of immediacy, presence and witness
that it had. Over 500 people listened intently to what the young
boy had written. It was a most memorable time of communicating.

Involved with WHO is communicating is also WHAT is communicated. For the
musician, as well as any life-artist, the communication must be one of
enthusiasm.

          En-thus-iasm comes from the Greek meaning: to be filled
          with God.

The musician's enthusiasm is communicating a rediscovering of the art of
music all over again. The music and the musician are one. Both communicate the relentless pursuit of perfection and the endurance to bring it
off. Both communicate the faith that is poured out and the love that is
to be shared between musician, music and the listener.

TO WHOM AM I COMMUNICATING?

Communication is genuine only when there is a reciprocal relationship
between the musician and the listener. Communication is always collaboration. There must be a shared enthusiasm for what is being heard.

          "I feel the crowd with me when I get that first hand as
          I get up on the stand, then it's up to me to play. The
          public's ready to give you a hand for anything you play
          good. Whatever you play - play it good."

                              Louis Armstrong
                              from THE LOUIS ARMSTRONG STORY, page 218

          "When the audience comprises mostly people that really
          listen, the standard of playing changes. There's
          always a relationship between the musicians and the
          audience. And when there was an audience reaction,
          you could feel that the music was almost pulled from
          you by this psychic rapport."

                              David Amram, composer, hornist
                              from VIBRATIONS, page 229

          "Most people mistakenly think that when they hear a
          piece of music, that they're not doing anything, but
          that something is being done to them. Now this is
          not true, and we must arrange our music, we must

arrange our art, we must arrange everything, I believe,
so that people realize that they themselves are doing it
and not that something is being done to them."

John Cage
from an interview

Listening is not something passive, but an action integral to the genuine-
ness of musical communication. What do people listen for? What kind of
sound will communicate most meaningfully? A musician, particularly one in
the church, must study what is needed and wanted in the community in order
that music may nurture the growth of the spirit of a people.

Too often, the musician in the church acts like this potentate in India:

> *"Once the Maharaja of Baroda, on hearing that healing*
> *could be accomplished through music, introduced concerts*
> *in certain hospitals and the amusing result was that all*
> *those who were suffering began to cry out, 'For God's*
> *sake, keep quiet! Go away!' That was not the music to*
> *soothe them. It only made them suffer more; it was like*
> *giving a stone for bread."*

from THE SUFI MESSAGE OF HAZRAT INAYAT KHAN
page 145

We climb onto the latest band wagon thinking that this is what the people
want and to our disillusionment find out that the complaint we thought we
were answering wasn't really the complaint in the first place.

Music, particularly the hymns of the church, is the <u>recitation of the
history of a people</u>. Music will define our roots, our ethnic heritage.
It will recall the struggles and suffering of a people as well as those
moments of triumph-in-spite-of-it-all.

We need to constantly ask, "Who are the people I am communicating with?
What are their needs? What is their history? What has meaning for
them? "

<u>Too often music in the church becomes meaningless and lifeless simply
because it has lost touch with the roots of life from which this people
springs.</u>

> I have heard church musicians rationalize their music for the
> congregation as something which will be "good" for the people.
> The musician acts like a druggist, prescribing what will cure
> the ills of the congregation provided that they will endure
> the medicinal music (which is often syrupy and sickeningly
> sweet). Other church musicians act as if they have a personal
> "educating vendetta" to lay on the congregation as they sit
> loftily in the choir loft rolling out music that is "correct."

27

Communication is neither a curing nor a correcting. It is communing, a coming together of spirits, a breaking of self-concerns and a pouring-out for others.

> "Sometimes this means that I have to listen to things that are important to you that I may not care a great deal about. Sometimes you'll have to do the same with me and you'll have to be patient with me. But both of us will need to know when something is important to the other so that we don't dismiss it."

Within recent years, the social recognition of ethnicity, heritage and people's culture have become increasingly more apparent in popular music as well as music composed for church use. The liturgy is starting to take seriously the meaning of people-ness in worship as we celebrate a people's heritage.

> The Chicago Daily News, August 10-11, 1974, ran a story with the headline: "POLKA MASS; Worship with a toe-tapping beat." The story told how Joe Cvek's polka band plays in a lounge and, on Saturday evenings, plays at the Resurrection Roman Catholic Church in Eveleth, Minnesota. The article described something about the church and its parishioners:

> > "The parishioners, for the most part, aren't new-fangled. Many of their fathers and grandfathers were Slovenian and Croatian immigrants who came from what is now Yugoslavia to work in the mines of the Mesabi Iron Range. They take their worship seriously.

> > "The church is packed. As a prelude to the mass, the band and choraleers offer a traditional Slovenian hymn. Worshippers join in as a few more people - young and old - try to make their way into the church.

> > "There is joy at a polka mass. When the worshippers finish singing a polka hymn, they are smiling. Sometimes, too, you'll see a few elderly men and women with tears in their eyes. The Old Country melodies mean a lot to them.

> > 'We all worked together, picking the songs, writing the lyrics, trying arrangements,' said Father Frank Perkovich, the pastor, 'but we couldn't be sure what the reaction would be.' After the first polka mass in May, 1973, the reaction was overwhelming. 'The people wanted a polka mass every week,' said Father Perkovich. 'But we had to keep it to every six weeks or so in order not to conflict with the band's nightclub dates."

Of course, the questions came up immediately: How do you explain a polka band in the choir loft — beer hall music in church?

Without hesitating, the priest replied: "What is sacred music? It's anything that raises your mind to God. It's anything that unites a congregation — the people and the priest — in praising God.

"These songs, these polkas and waltzes, have been cherished by generations of Slovenian and Croation people. The music is beautiful. It reaches our hearts. So I asked myself, 'Why couldn't we change the theme of some of the ballads to convey a religious message?'"

The thrust of communication is not for the blame or admonition of the hearer, rather, it is the communicator's hope that the hearer will become the witness-bearer and go and tell the story. This will effectively happen when the sounds, the music and spoken words are rooted in the living history of a people.

Genuine communication senses the pulse of the people.

WHY AM I COMMUNICATING ?

What motivates a musician to play before others is often an intangible quality. Sometimes we have a personal need to be with a community of people, in a musical role. Hopefully, the motivating energy of the musician who plays in the church will be more than someone who wants to "present" some sounds or a lyric. The church musician is to be a transparency; a ministry through music that opens us all up to the workings of God in the world.

The musician must learn to get beyond himself or herself, in order to get across to the people. You may be nervous before you play. You must learn to go beyond your own nervousness. If there are technically difficult places in the music, you must prepare those places harder than the other parts of the material. You must prepare the best way you can so that you can enjoy the creating of the music at the moment when you are making it.

I once studied trumpet with Gene Shaw, who had worked with the Charlie Mingus Jazz Workshop in New York. I'll never forget our first session:

Gene told me not to bring out my horn because we wouldn't be playing this first time. He told me to sit on the edge of a chair and relax. Then he told me something that has stayed with me for a long time:

"You are your own greatest obstacle to getting your ideas
out through the horn. You can master technique, your
fingers can play the notes, but until you and the instrument are one, you'll never fully express yourself like you
can."

He then guided me through a "sensing tour" asking me to
use my imagination and "feel" my toes and feet, then my
legs, stomach area, chest, arms, shoulders and head. He
recommended this as an exercise before starting to practice. It was a method for preparing myself to play more
expressively and creatively and to communicate what I
was feeling inside.

The musician in the church is one who is freed-up in Spirit and ability
to pour out what's inside through the music that is played. The creative musician holds nothing back but gives himself completely to the
moment and to the opportunity that is present. It is in the act of
pouring out myself that I will find myself and receive back from others
more than I gave away.

The art of communication is basically a searching for the you to commune
with the me until both of us become we. Communication is always a two-
way movement. Without the listener, the musician's work is only a monologue, not a dialogue. And when communication happens between people,
something very special and mysterious takes place:

there is a oneness that forms between the lives that
participate. There is a communion between personal
lives. We give by receiving and we receive from others
as we give to them. Alone, a person is quite a bit less
than what he or she could be. But in communication, in
openness to another, the possibility of unlimited growth
is offered.

We are never Self-alone. We are always Self-in-relation-
to other Selves. It is in the giving beyond our Self
that invokes a freedom for others who respond by going
outside of themselves.

"What motivates me to play music in praise of God and before God's
People?" is a question that needs to be asked and answered daily. You
may need to take a few moments of quiet time and really pray or meditate
on what you hope to do in the next half-hour of your practicing time.
You may need to speak a simple prayer before you play:

"Lord, make me an instrument of your peace." (St. Francis)

and then pour yourself out for God's glory that you and the congregation
might become one.

HOW I COMMUNICATE MY STYLE

The way you communicate an idea is often as important as the idea itself.
Each person has a particular style of getting ideas across. This is true
verbally as well as musically.

Often the way you introduce a new piece of music will have a lot to do
with the way the listener receives it.

> For example, in workshops one question keeps coming up
> again and again: "How do you share a new piece of music
> with the congregation?" The problem is not with the music,
> generally, but with finding the right words or sounds which
> open the people to participating in the experience.
>
> Imagine how uninviting it would be to have someone stand
> in front of the congregation and, with much self-
> consciousness, stammer: "Well, this is a new song, we
> haven't had much time to practice it, but we hope you like
> it and try to sing along with us whenever you can." I've
> been to some worship services where that was the style of
> the music; self-conscious and not very sure.
>
> Or there's the other style of the command. "We will now
> sing hymn number 362!" The direction is not one that is
> particularly inviting, but it leaves you no other choice.
> There's too much of this kind of commanding rhetoric
> going on in worship that does nothing to facilitate
> warmth or love with the people. Slogans like "CELEBRATE
> LIFE!" or "REJOICE!" have done more to hinder the genu-
> ineness of a release of joy in worship. They have become
> so over-used that they no longer mean anything.
>
> From my experience, I've learned that a language of in-
> vitation is most productive in involving others in a shared
> experience of music and worship. Rather than giving a com-
> mand to sing, you might try inviting the people with a
> question: "Would you join me in singing...?" Share some
> of the history of how that song came to be written. In
> that sharing, people get to know something about the music
> and something about what you feel is important.

Your style of communication is your own _personal_ _forming_ of ideas and
sharing them with others. The way you choose to do this will reveal
your personality, your spirit that resists being pinned down, your
discipline and your hopes.

THE WHERE AND WHEN
OF COMMUNICATING

Every act of communication is situational. Every time we communicate
it is a new time in history. For that reason there is always the element of uniqueness and world premiere whenever we speak. It is a
tragedy, therefore, when we waste time or leave that new time empty
by "saying or playing nothing" or filling the space with something
that has become lifeless and meaningless. There is a timeliness to
everything and we must develop a sensitivity to sense the moment and
the appropriateness of what we communicate.

> A minister's wife wrote a hymn about the prison conditions
> she heard and read about at Attica. The hymn was sung on
> the Sunday following the week of rioting at that prison.
> There was a great sense of the historic moment in that hymn.
> It was obviously the right words to sing at the right time.
> The song was sung once and never sung again.

We need to understand that not all hymns need to be eternal. They may
not even be "great" in an enduring way. Their gift of being momentary
will be in their power to speak of the present situation and to articulate the feelings of the people who gather.

Repeatability and endurance may be qualities of mass production but they
are not necessarily desireable in creative music and worship. The creative situation is nourished by the meaning of the moment. Being in the
right place at the right time and saying the appropriate thing is a
quality that needs to be encouraged everywhere, particularly in the
church.

It is the same with the musician: if people feel that what is being played
at that particular time could be played at any other time and result in a
similar experience, then a kind of deadliness falls over the people. Creative music, by its very nature, is not repeatable. It will be a new expression every time it is played. If the music of the church becomes mere
repetition of what we've heard before, then we are leaving the newness of
lifetime empty.

> Mahalia Jackson resided on the South-side of Chicago.
> When she died, a Catholic church in Hyde Park held a
> special mass celebrating her Spirit. For the benediction,
> a recording of her singing "Bless This House" was used
> as the church bells tolled. The choice of song, place
> in the liturgy and timeliness in history made that re-
> cording a most memorable experience. When could a re-
> cording have been so moving? To try to repeat the event
> at another time would not have held as much significance.

WHERE an event happens will influence the effectiveness of the communication.

> During the March on Washington which Dr. Martin Luther King, Jr. directed, Marian Anderson sang on the steps of the Washington Monument to thousands of listeners. A few blocks away, Mahalia Jackson sang Gospel songs on a street corner to a few hundred listeners. Both singers were tremendous and the words they sang were great. But on that day, the place influenced the gathering of the historic moment.

> My ordination to a ministry of celebration within the United Church of Christ was one in which I would be going beyond the limits of any one denomination. I knew that to be ordained in a church building would be a contradiction to what I was preparing for, so I rented the Museum of Contemporary Art in Chicago and held the event there. The museum, as a place, symbolized our concern for the future and the communicative power of art. The ordination site brought together the elements of my ministry: a concern for culture, the artist's visionary ability to see beyond the time present, and the calling to ministry to a world in need of new visions.

The PLACE or environment where something happens will communicate the style of the person or musical group.

> Leo Beranek, who designed the Lincoln Center in New York, observed: ".... it seems clear that today's listeners prefer particular kinds of acoustical spaces for performances of music of particular styles."

> from MUSIC, ARCHITECTURE, ACOUSTICS
> page 43

We need to help people broaden their understanding of PLACE and SPACE in the church so that we are not prejudiced against folk, rock or jazz music simply because we have associated these styles with the coffeehouse, concert or dance halls. Music goes beyond the limitations of cultural space. The only guideline we need to use is the question: "How appropriate is the music for our people, for the time we live in and for the meaning of the moment?"

We need to learn how to use the place where something happens to enhance the musical expression, rather than limit it. Many of our early religious choral compositions, particularly plainchant, were written to be performed in reverberant cathedrals. When these kinds of compositions are performed in an acoustically dead environment they suffer from the

lack of fullness and lose much of their power. Many composers of the
plainsong style would write for the environment. They would put in
rests in the music so as to emphasize the after-ring of the building.

The creative musician needs to be aware of the acoustics of the room in
which the music will be performed. With careful listening and imagination, different styles of music can be introduced into the congregation's life that will be enhanced by the space.

Mobility is a key to the use of space in many churches. Having freedom
to move around, to process in and out of the sanctuary, are charac-
teristics of the church. Later in the book we will explore the possibilities of mobility for instrumentalists, choirs, soloists and the
congregation as a means of making better use of the space in which
worship takes place.

Rev. Paul Stiffler officiating at Kent Schneider's ordination at Chicago
playing trumpet with the jazz ensemble. His vest was created from leather
border of fringe on the vest.

PART TWO

MUSIC AND THE LITURGY

seum of Contemporary Art, June 8, 1970. Kent is seen in the background
Sr. Adelaide. Symbols of a ministry of celebration were attached to a

35

MUSIC and the CHURCH: 1957-1976

In the '40's and the '50's, church music was exploring the past for material that would have meaning for the local congregation. As theologians continued the historical quest for Jesus, the country was mindful of a growing war in Europe and, later, Korea. The threat of communism in America made people in the church suspicious of anything but the tried and true.

Musically, this period meant that the Roman Catholics would be listening to the Latin Mass with plainsong, polyphonic music and Gregorian chants. The Lutherans would be singing the hymns of Luther and the chorales of Bach. The Methodists uncovered the works of John and Charles Wesley. The Congregational churches made much of the Pilgrim traditions. The Brethren and other denominations rallied around their hymnals. This opportunity to reclaim the past made all of the religious communities aware of commonly shared histories. We really weren't that far apart, nor were our styles of worship that different. The roots of ecumenicity were beginning to take hold.

In a time of conformity, the church music of the past was pleasing and comfortable. But, did it mean anything to the people who sang it? In the '50's, and finally reaching a zenith during the late '60's, people in the pews and some church musicians began to feel that the music of the past was not going to make worship meaningful in a slowly evolving society. Also, during the '50's, we had the beginnings of a popular music that the youth of the time could claim as their own, primarily because the adults didn't want to have anything to do with it. With this simultaneous growth of music among the young and the feeling that the old church music of the past was being sung with declining inspiration, we have the gulf opening up between what's vital in the culture and what's proper in the church.

With the maturing of the new music, from the seeds of rock 'n roll and the folk songs, young people (under the magical age barrier of 30) took the music as a means of personal identification, as a sign of independence from adults and as an expression of their inner feelings. Combined with the awareness that young people were not participating in the church, the scene was set for the planting of new seeds of church music.

THE SEEDS ARE SOWN: 1957-1962

With the research being done into the history of the church's music, people began to find out that some of the most sacred of the hymn tunes originated in the not-so-sacred saloons and drinking establishments of the day. It was a common practice for composers to utilize the popular melodies of the time when writing hymns and cantatas. Well, why couldn't we also do the same — take popular melodies and idioms of the people's music — and incorporate the sounds into the worship service?

Among the first to try was Father Geoffrey Beaumont (born 1904). He is an Anglican priest who tried setting hymns to popular tunes while he was serving as a chaplain during World War II. In the spring of 1957, his 20th Century Folk Mass (Fiesta, FLP 25000) was premiered in Providence, Rhode Island. It was played by a 45-piece orchestra and was sung by 12 voices. It's Gershwinesque style of composition and it's Broadway sound were probably very revolutionary at the time.

Beaumont defined his use of the term "folk music" as being the "normal, everyday, popular melodies and rhythms enjoyed and understood by the majority of men and women in Britain today. It is part of their cultural background. The music heightens the dramas they watch in cinemas or on television. The idiom expresses their sentiments and emotions. To use this idiom in churches is to go back to the days when 'religion' and 'life' were merely aspects of the same social existence."

An article about the Folk Mass appeared in the May, 1957 issue of Music Americana (77:6) applauding the effort as a way of encouraging the congregation to take a fuller part in the Mass by responding to the cantor and by singing back his phrases. The article also mentioned the high attraction that such music had for teen-agers. Included in the Mass were three hymns set to new tunes: "There's A Wideness In God's Mercy," "Now Thank We All Our God" and "Lord, Thy Word Abideth."

The first major use of liturgical jazz was developed by Ed Summerlin, a saxophonist and composer. In 1958, he wrote "Requiem For Mary Jo" — an expression of his feelings over the death of his nine-month old daughter. In 1959, working with Roger Ortmayer, professor of Christianity and the Arts at Perkins School of Theology in Dallas, Ed composed a jazz setting of John Wesley's Order of Morning Prayer, recorded as Liturgical Jazz (Ecclesia, ER 101). It is interesting to note that this beginning grew out of a historically-centered liturgy; again, a characteristic of where the church was at. This work premiered at the National Convocation of Methodist Youth held at Purdue University, West Lafayette, Indiana, on August 28, 1959.

Dr. Ross Snyder, professor at The Chicago Theological Seminary, was part of a panel assembled following the premier experience. In 1967, I found a tape marked "Snyder and Jazz — West Lafayette." It was stuffed in some old files that were going to be thrown out.

I filed the tape away, only to listen to it in its entirety in late 1975. I realized that it contained reactions and discussion about the Summerlin setting of the Order of Morning Prayer. From what I could gather, these comments were part of a plenary session which included teams of clergy and young people who had participated in the jazz setting. Here is some of the conversation:

Man: "We do not feel enough in worship. Jazz has made me feel like I've never felt before (audience laughter). Remember that the feeling level is hard to verbalize, so bear with me. Two weeks ago I attended a jazz festival in Chicago and was really moved at that time. This week it has been the same. I felt more of a whole person as I've had this feeling level restored to me. Now, I'm sure there are theological implications to this."

Ross: "If you're in kind of a mood of despair, would you get more help by listening to the blues or by listening to, for instance, 'O Sacred Head Now Wounded'? Which has the greatest power of vocalizing and helping you become aware of the real depths of despair?"

Man: "Speaking from last night's experience, I would say that Odetta singing the song about not being able to have love returned was just as moving as the Bach anthem that was played last night."

Woman: "I'm speaking from my own feelings, and I'm being highly critical of this convocation. I speak as a young adult counselor and as a church musician. My feeling is that in the 17th and 18th centuries we didn't take the popular secular music and move it into the church. Why do we move in jazz, which, at this point, is not the high religious music of the church? In other words, it's not the contemporary modern form. This jazz is old stuff. It's not contemporary or modern, as compared with Charles Ives or Stravinsky or Schoenberg."

Ross: "You're speaking for modern music and not just jazz?"

Woman: "Yes!"

Ross: "How do you answer, then, the people who point out, correctly, that Martin Luther and people of the Reformation did go into the popular music of their day, even into the saloons of their time, and took out the drinking songs and made them into the deepest religious chorales that we have?"

Woman: "Because some of the greatest music doesn't always come from the church, no matter what the words say."

Ross: "You don't think jazz has this possibility and that modern music does?"

Woman: "I think jazz has the possibility, but some of the jazz we've been hearing has been downright corny."

Clergyman: "Jazz is not the Gospel. It's an expression by the musicians. We can only get out of jazz what the musicians feel and witness. It's sad that some of the youth are going away from here thinking that they can find God in secular jazz."

Youth: "I attended the Morning Prayer service. I personally did not like the jazz when the minister was speaking his sermon. But, during the other parts of the service, I found that the jazz, when we were reading, gave a tendency for us to bring out certain points in the reading rather than reading in dull tones. We put more feeling into it. Rather than reading just with our eyes, we were reading with our hearts."

Ross: "The morning that I attended, the drums really spoke to me. I must admit that a muted saxophone does not speak to me of the Christian faith."

Man: "Some of the youth were talking about the headlines in the paper: 'Methodist Youth Jazzing It Up — Ministers Don't Dig It.' They really felt that most of the ministers really don't understand what's going on. From some of the comments I've been hearing, I'm inclined to agree. I suspect that some of the times when we ministers say that these kids are mixed up, it's really a reflection of our own situation."

Participant: "Some of us feel that we're putting too much emphasis on the jazz rather than looking through it and seeing what it brings into our lives. Another comment from my youth was that the music hit them the wrong way in thinking of hearing this music flow through the doors of our churches and into the streets. We wondered what effect this music would have on passers-by who don't come to church. But, the music the church is using now doesn't bring them in either, so, something's got to change somewhere."

Student: "How can we combine the words of Wesley's old English with contemporary forms of music? If we use 'hip' music of today, we should use the 'cool' language of today. I can't see any need to modernize God."

Ross: "Let me articulate what might be some principles for us:

We do not want to make young people the victims of so-called 'popular culture' by what has been done here. There's a difference between jazz as the top people are trying to develop it and the kind of material played on the radio. Jazz, at its best, is a time when the musicians are together and something deep inside them gets expressed. Jazz is an episodic thing of the moment. It is a one-shot moment of truth."

Summerlin reflected back upon that 1959 experience in an article written for the Liturgical Conference in 1967:

"In 1959, I wrote a jazz service for the church. After all the furor had died down, I settled down to try to figure out what had been accomplished. One of the things appeared to be that the church could now open its doors to contemporary music in a definitely secular mode. This, of course, went hand in hand with the message that the contemporary theologians were preaching; we cannot separate the sacred from the secular, and, if God does dwell within us, it is an on-going thing that does not come and go depending on whether we are in church or not. What we have forgotten is that most Protestant church music came from

40

secular sources and that our classical European church musical forms emerged from early dance suites. So, I continued on my way, trying to find a style of music that would have artistic integrity and still lend itself to corporate worship."

The uncertain mood of the church was characterized by a report in the March 2, 1960 issue of The Christian Century. The article, entitled "It Was Worship Even Though It Was Jazz," was critical of an hour-long television broadcast of "Requiem For Mary Jo" on the 20th of February. Describing the program as a "thought-provoking presentation of a Methodist church service," noting that "it differed from others in that the musical language was that of jazz," the writer criticized the "lazy, monotonous drum-brush" as "an effect-worker" and the words and music which "seldom attained a speaking acquaintance."

The real gripe was with the jazz language itself. "Jazz still bears connotations and importations which do not serve the church well." However, if jazz "is offered with reverence, it may become a language of the soul."

In an article appearing later in The Christian Century (March 23, 1960), which was entitled "Jazz At The Altar?", Elwyn A. Wienandt, a teacher at Baylor University in Waco, Texas, proposed that introducing secular musical idioms into the church was nothing new. It was a phenomenon with deeply-rooted historical precedent.

The point was made that "superficially, it would seem that the use of the jazz idiom in a worship service of our time should be no less acceptable than other musical idioms of past centuries. However, the close identification of jazz, in the eyes of many observers, with exuberant forms of secular entertainment... has made it an intruder that is guilty by association. If the musical style of jazz can be assimilated into an area of our lives that is marked by dignity, tradition and solemnity (or at least restrained enthusiasm), it stands a chance of being recognized as an enduring feature."

The author recognized that jazz can be meaningful only when it loses its previous identification. However, "at the moment (jazz) achieves such a release of identification, it will very likely have lost its vitality, for the very thing that makes it exciting, vital and readily identifiable outside the church, stands as the greatest barrier to its acceptance within."

By 1961, some churches were hosting "Jazz Vespers" which were generally without any set liturgical form. Often the musicians would improvise on a church tune. The Rev. Canon Standrod T. Carmichael of the staff of Christ Church Cathedral in St. Louis, Missouri, and Rev. John Gensel, a Lutheran minister in New York City, initiated jazz vespers in their communities. Carmichael composed <u>Music For The Liturgy</u> (TRAV 18228) an Anglican setting. It consisted of Kyrie, Sanctus, Agnus Dei and Gloria in English texts and was sung by the choir with the congregation, accompanied by a jazz quintet. It was written for congregational singing rather than concert performance. The unison melodic lines made this a very usable setting and offered improvisational opportunities for the musicians.

In 1962, Summerlin had composed a work called "Evensong" which premiered at the Episcopal Church of the Ephiphany as the closing event of a four-day jazz festival in Washington, D.C. William Robert Miller describes some of the service:

> "The processional and the refrain of the recessional hymn were sung by the congregation and were written in simple ballad style to a text by the Rev. John G. Harrel, with this in mind. Following a relaxed instrumental prelude, soloists improvised unobtrusively as the processional was sung. Later, preceding the congregational reading of the Apostles' Creed, choir and instrumentalists performed a motet, "Song of the Apostles" with words beginning: 'Glory on that mountain, glory all around, glory be to Jesus, let's make a sound' — clearly of gospel-blues derivation. The offertory was an instrumental work composed in modified twelve-tone style with opportunities for improvisation — an excellent blend of advanced classical and jazz idioms."

<u>The World of Pop Music and Jazz,</u>
pages 89-90

RELIGIOUS JAZZ RECORDED

During this period, prominent jazz musicians were starting to record religious compositions and arrangements as part of their albums.

- Thelonious Monk recorded <u>Monk's Music</u> with an arrangement of one of his favorite hymns "Abide With Me", featuring John Coltrane, Coleman Hawkins, Ray Copeland, Gigi Gryce. Riverside RLP 12-242 (6-26-57).

- Charlie Mingus recorded "Revelations/1st Movement" — a "celebrated evocation of the Deity" which "has already assumed considerable rank in historical jazz moments." On <u>Outstanding Jazz Compositions of the</u>

20th Century (6-20-57) Columbia C2L 31. Mingus also
recorded "Wednesday Night Prayer Meeting" and Bobby
Timmons' "Moanin'" (Atlantic 1305), "Prayer For Passive
Resistance" (Mercury 20627) and "Ecclusiasticus" (Atlantic 1377).

- Mary Lou Williams, pianist and veteran jazz stylist,
  abandoned a playing career in 1954 to enter a long
  period of prayer and meditation. She was convinced
  that her talents should be used to spread good, re-
  gardless of the way the world might interpret those
  talents. "The ability to play jazz is a gift from God,"
  she said. "This music is based on the spirituals —
  it's our only American art form — and should be played
  everywhere, including the church." She composed a jazz
  hymn to St. Martin de Porres, entitled "Black Christ of
  the Andes" and other works, "Anima Christi" and "Praise
  The Lord". By 1967, she would be featured in concert
  at Carnegie Hall, playing religious jazz.

- Donald Byrd, trumpeter and son of a Detroit minister,
  began featuring religious tunes on his albums, beginning in 1961 with "Amen" on Fuego (Blue Note 4026) and
  Hush" on Royal Flush (Blue Note 4101) and "Pentecostal
  Feeling" on Free Form (Blue Note ST-84118). By late
  1962 or early 1963, Donald had finished a modern version
  of church traditional music with polyphonic writing,
  harmonic backing with voices and jazz instrumentation.
  A New Perspective (Blue Note BLP-4124) featured Byrd's
  spiritual-like pieces, a new approach to the Afro-
  American religious heritage.

- John Lewis, composer and pianist with MJQ premiered
  Original Sin (Atlantic 1370) in 1961 as a ballet score
  to scenes from Genesis.

- Duke Ellington had composed the concert work Black,
  Brown and Beige in 1943 when it was performed at
  Carnegie Hall. Included in the work were two fine
  religious pieces "Come Sunday" and a setting on the
  23rd Psalm. These were later recorded by Mahalia
  Jackson (Columbia CL 1162). The "Come Sunday" theme
  would become the basis for Ellington's first Concert
  of Sacred Music in 1965.

The seeds were growing, along with the awakening consciousness of
the Negro and the rights of freedom. To a great extent, the church
was both birthing place and training ground for many of the jazz
musicians and vocalists. The church was also the meeting place
for the civil rights and freedom movement in this country.

Perhaps, for these musicians, their pioneering expressions of the spirit became part of that on-rush towards freedom: a freedom through religious expression; a freedom from physical bonds and injustice; a freedom ultimately in the one event which makes all men equal — death itself.

> "If the Negro will ever achieve the dignity and civil authenticity that he deserves, it will be because he has a vision of himself as a child of God, free before God and, therefore, worthy of respect and love and justice by men who stand before God in the same way. The Negro has given this vision to the world of jazz, and though that world has tampered with the heritage at times, still at its roots is the conviction of the dignity of man and his freedom."

Father Norman J. O'Connor
"Thoughts on the Liturgy and Jazz"
from <u>Jazz Suite on the Mass Texts</u>

FREEDOM AND FERMENT: 1963-1969

It is significant that this period of growth was nurtured by the Ecumenical Spirit of the Vatican II Council, and that the first document approved by that Council was the Constitution on the Sacred Liturgy. Pope Paul said, "the liturgy was the first subject to be examined and the first, too, in a sense, in intrinsic worth and in importance for the life of the Church." There was a new sense of freedom "even in the liturgy, the Church has no wish to impose a rigid uniformity in matters which do not involve the faith or the good of the whole community. Rather, she respects and fosters the spiritual adornments and gifts of the various races and peoples." (Article 37)

The Constitution devoted an entire chapter to the place of music in the liturgy and spoke of the Church's musical tradition as being of "immeasurable value" (Article 112) which is to be "observed and fostered with very great care" (Article 114). The church acknowledged Gregorian chant as proper to the Roman liturgy, though "other kinds of sacred music are by no means excluded from liturgical celebration" (Article 116). The document also noted that musical traditions of other people in other lands often "play a great part in their religious and social life. For this reason, due importance is to be attached to their music" (Article 119). No longer were Western styles of church music going to be imposed on a people. The times demanded that each culture establish its natural and peculiar identity.

So, during this period, we start getting a number of Mass settings from other parts of the world. Notably, <u>Missa Bantu</u> (Philips PCC 211) and <u>Missa Luba</u> (Philips PCC 219-619), <u>Misa del Cante Grande</u> (Polydor 512-SFIT), <u>Misa Flamenca</u> (Philips PCC 843-137-PY) and <u>Misa Panamerica</u> (Discos ALELUYA A-015) expressed the music of the Spanish and Mexican communities; <u>Misa Gitana</u> (London International GH 46005-56005) was a gypsy Mass; <u>Misa ala Chilena</u> (Odon EMI LOM 8186) was a Chile Mass; and <u>Misa Folklorica Columbiana</u> (ORB OB-ST-0020) was a Mass from Columbia.

MORE THAN THAN THE ORGAN:
Instrumental Alternatives

The Constitution stated that while the organ was still "held in high esteem," other instruments could also be used in worship, provided that "the instruments are suitable for sacred use, or can be made so, that they accord with the dignity of the temple and truly contribute to the edification of the faithful" (Article 120).

> "I believe that no matter what the skill of a drummer or saxophonist, if this is the thing he does best, and he offers it sincerely from the heart in, or as an accompaniment of his worship, then it will not be unacceptable because of the instrument upon which he makes his demostration."

> Duke Ellington

Martin Marty, church historian, writing in <u>The Christian Century</u> (March 23, 1960), observed that "instrumental music lacks a verbal referent, having no recognizable story or root-event; hence it has usually found its home in the church by means of its connotations. Music from the distant past, from what we call an age of faith, seems to belong in the church even though it may once have had a secular connotation, for, then, it seems the sacred and the secular inter-penetrated and overlapped significantly. Atonal music, born in our century, is at best regarded ambivalently, somewhat like a step-child, by the church in our world come of age. What acceptance today's music has found in the church is largely in the area of choral or organ music, as opposed to instrumental music for worship."

Church musicians were generally defensive about admitting other instruments into the musical life of the church. From 1964-1969, there was a constant give and take among the church organists and the youthful folk musicians turned church musicians. It was a showdown in many churches; the guitar verses the organ. The instruments became symbolic of the culture and where the church was going:

the organ is an instrument which is powerful, large and immobile. It is symbolic of an immutable and unfathomable world, the world of the holy. One author notes that the organ music in the church is of the quality of a "religious adagio"— slow, grave, melancholy, nostolgic, communicating a minor sound, sadness and a "mystery" that is not precisely the paschal mystery and decidely of a senile spirituality.

The guitar is an instrument which is mobile, which invites the voice to sing and needs to be strummed again and again in order to sustain a note or chord. The guitar became part of the counter culture. (Note, on the cover of Roszak's The Making of a Counter Culture, that the youth is carrying a guitar.) To play the guitar loud and with sharp sounds was a way of talking back to a screaming world.

Guitar "folk Masses" became the new thing for the time of church renewal in the mid-'60's. Those who had predicted that the use of jazz or folk music would be a one-shot event in most churches were realizing that a revolution in the sounds of religious music was starting to grow.

> "While the humble guitar is unlikely to replace the majestic king of instruments, we might recall at this moment in the ever-changing history of musical styles the honored place of the guitar in human experience. It has served as an outlet for the sincere feeling of countless ordinary people as well as interpreter of exalted classical music."
>
> Dr. Paul E. Elbin, American Guild of Organists
> from THE HYMN, January 1970

TO BEAT or NOT TO BEAT,
That Was the Question

On April 18, 1966, the U.S. Bishops' Commission on the Liturgical Apostalate announced that "the needs of the faithful of a particular cultural background or of a particular age level may often be met by a music that can serve as a congenial, liturgically orientated expression of prayer." It should be recognized that "different groupings of the faithful assembled in worship respond to different styles of musical expression."

The faithful did respond. Newspapers and denominational magazines began printing articles either for or against the use of folk, jazz and rock in the church.

NEW SONGS UNTO THE LORD (<u>SATURDAY REVIEW</u>, April 10, 1965)

COOL CREEDS (<u>TIME</u> Magazine, July 9, 1965)

SACRED MUSIC IN CHANGE (<u>AMERICA</u>, February 12, 1966)

DEMURRER ON JAZZ LORD'S SUPPERS (<u>THE CHRISTIAN CENTURY</u>,
                                    June 22, 1966)

CHURCH MUSIC REVOLUTION GAINING (<u>CHICAGO DAILY NEWS</u>,
                                    July 23, 1966)

JAZZ GOES TO CHURCH (<u>EBONY</u> Magazine, 1966)

<u>'Beat Mass' or Mess? - 3 Combos in Rome Chapel</u> (1966)

> Three mop-haired youth combos banged out a
> "beat mass" in a Roman Catholic chapel
> Wednesday night. Listeners couldn't agree
> whether it was a howling success or a holy
> mess. A crowd of 500....stomped their feet
> and bobbed their heads to the rhythm of the
> electric guitars, drums, organ and singers.
> Another 1,000 outside beat on the door trying
> to get in.

A Dominican priest opened the concert with this explanation:

> "In a hard and merciless era like ours, a pro-
> fane music can be useful in expressing reli-
> gious sentiments — although I want to assure
> you that the promoters of this enterprise
> (Oratorian Fathers, a religious order speciali-
> zing in youth work) have absolutely no intention
> of putting light music into the church's official
> cult, that is, its worship."

Then, on January 4, 1967, headlines read: "POPE FORBIDS JAZZ
MASSES." However, the official document that came from Rome
(Congregation of Rites and the Commission for the Application
of Vatican Council II's Constitution on the Sacred Liturgy)
deplored certain "almost incredible" liturgical celebrations
publicized in "news items and photographs." The only mention
of music that appeared in the document was in a sentence concerned with "Masses offered using strange and arbitrary rites,
vestments and formulas and sometimes accompanied by music of
a totally profane and worldly character, not worthy of a
sacred action." The style of music was never mentioned.

On March 7, 1967, the newspaper headlines stated: "POPE APPROVES OF JAZZ TUNES AT SERVICES"; "POPE OPENS WAY FOR JAZZ SPIRITUALS IN MASS"; "POPE APPROVES MODERNIZED MUSIC IN MASS."

The document, entitled "Instruction on Music in the Liturgy," was considered a landmark in modernizing the rules for Catholic church music. The papal document called for "more singing in services," permission to translate Latin hymns into modern languages, recommended "the use of instruments native to individual countries and cultures" and authorized a "period of wide experimentation to adapt modern musical forms and compositions to church use."

"Beat music and jazz were not mentioned specifically. But, there was no prohibition against them, and the document said new musical modes should be 'held in honor, encouraged and used as the occasion demands.'" (Chicago Daily News, March 7, 1967)

Leading priests at the Institute of Sacred Music in Rome could not say what kinds of music could be permitted or what would be condemned. One priest was quoted as saying: "We are in a period of transition."

Bob Dylan told us "The Times Are A-Changin'." The scene was set for a growing and struggling creative period.

> "The subject of liturgical music is...neither simple
> nor unimportant. Perhaps nowhere in our liturgical
> renewal must greater flexibility and a range of free-
> dom and experimentation be allowed. For music, in
> order to be functional, must be constantly related
> to the people whom it is to serve — the individual
> congregation or group, with varying levels of age,
> cultural sophistication, background. Music suitable
> for one group may prove not as suitable for another.
> Here trained judgment, rather than a multi-licity of
> regulations, is called for. There can be no pat
> formulas, at least not at our present stage of
> growth."
>
> C. J. McNaspy, S.J.
> from Our Changing Liturgy
> page 135

With no "pat formulas" the liturgical music of this time was in a muddle. Certainly one cause was the feeling that religious music had to be something distinctive from secular music. Somehow, church musicians felt that there must be some particular mold into which music could be poured before it was good enough to be sung or played to the praise of God. Who within the church would direct us in setting the criteria for "religious music"? Who

would help us discriminate between the secular and the sacred?
When the church was confronted with a decision during this period,
it deferred giving answer and returned to the "tradition." And,
so, the Catholic community rejoiced in the Gregorian chants and
the Protestants found the hymns of Wesley and Luther very comfortable. It was a period in which religion sought to keep the
world out of the sanctuary. Ministers were told to preach about
the scriptures, not about social issues. The people inside the
church had forgotten what Christ's Body was all about.

Growing outside of the church was a cultural upheaval of young
people, folk music, rock music, protest music, civil rights
marches, a growing distrust of big government, an unpopular
war in Vietnam and liberation movements for women, Blacks,
Chicanos and Indians. Yet, the church's liturgy tried to maintain itself with proper dignity and reverence. Orderliness in
liturgics seemed more important than responsiveness to the needs
of the people.

> "A liturgy whose exclusive preoccupation seems to be
> with its development, away from man's creative involve-
> ment in other areas of life, cannot call itself espe-
> cially "Christian." We need a basic revision of our
> liturgy if it is not to alienate men by cutting them
> off from the world. The specific forms with which
> most of us have to live have taken on an alienating
> character which has contributed to the separation of
> liturgical life from everyday life."
>
> Evangelista Vilanova, O.S.B.
> from The Crisis of Liturgical Reform
> page 11

The Protestants also began sensing how out of touch with life the
liturgy had become. Even new music set into the old format would
be deadly. A total re-thinking of liturgy and music was needed.
Malcolm Boyd, an Episcopalian priest, was one of the strong voices
of the mid-'60's, calling for renewal in the church. In an article
entitled "The Ecumenical Freedom Body — A Call To The People",
Boyd set the challenge of the times:

> "It is the people who must now seize the church. The
> people must affirm...in a revolutionary expression...
> the common ministry of the people of God. The people
> must remake worship. This will involve a number of
> painful and wonderful changes. As a result, people will
> be able to worship honestly with their bodies, minds
> and souls. The people will not wait for a commission on
> worship to hold some meetings, issue some reports, make

a report on the reports at a big conference for reports
and then publish a seasonable break-through book. The
renewal must come from the bottom, for the top is insu-
lated, fearful and even lacking in the required dynamics.
This renewal of worship, at the bottom, needs to be a
grassroots affair; lively, radical, indigenous, NOW.

"New hymns can appear, not from a hymnal commission
operating in a peopleless ghetto, but from congregations
of the people."

"The peoples need freedom," was a sign scrawled on a wall in
Mississippi in 1965, as part of the rights movement. The writing
was now on the walls of the church. What was happening in the
society was about to start happening in the churches. We were
being called to a thorough honesty and uncompromising stand for
the rights of people to determine their own destiny. Would the
music of the church support that determination?

THE FLOWERING OF FOLK

Folk music grew with the people. It mirrored their concern for
human rights, their feeling of alienation and of being thrown
into social situations that they did not create. The music
sounded the times of searching for something to hold on to.
Pete Seeger, Paul Simon, Bob Dylan, Phil Ochs, Joan Baez and
Buffy Saint-Marie were some of the composer-singers who gave us
the words to accompany the marches of the '60's.

Intimacy was a characteristic of the folk song. Singing to a
small group of people in a coffee house became a standard environment in the early '60's. Then, as some songs grew in
popularity, they moved from the small rooms to the concert stage
and to the top of the record charts. On most college campuses,
you could find some look-a-like trio singing the songs of Peter,
Paul and Mary, the New Christy Minstrels or the Kingston Trio.

The church was also listening to the popular folk music. High
school students were playing guitars as part of their social
maturation process. "Hootenannies" and "sing-alongs" were ways
of entertaining with the new music of folk. There was a warm,
friendly spirit associated with the music, a characteristic
that many young people found lacking in the adult dominated
church.

At first, the churches started to appropriate some of the songs
as replacements for the hymns. "Blowin' In The Wind", "Sounds
of Silence" and "Bridge Over Troubled Water" were among the most
popular folk songs which the church sang in the mid-'60's. Then,
with the encouragement of the Catholic Church, priests, nuns and
seminarians began composing Mass settings and hymns in a style
of folk music. Among these composers were:

- Reverend Clarence Rivers, who began writing music in the
  late '50's in the style of the Black spiritual, was concerned about the integration of the Afro-American culture
  into the life of the Catholic church; particularly for
  the Black Catholic community. He composed an American
  Mass Program (World Library), one of the first English
  settings, in 1964 and The Brotherhood of Man Mass (World
  Library), which was featured at the Newport Jazz Festival in 1965. He is one of the most creative liturgist-
  musicians at work today, integrating religious music,
  the spirit of life and liturgical renewal in this
  country. He is most concerned about striving for a
  quality of artistic integrity in the Mass as well as
  drawing upon the genius of the Black community. Father
  River's music and recordings are available from Stimuli
  Incorporated, Box 20066, Cincinnati, Ohio 45220.

- Ray Repp was a student at Kendrick Seminary in St. Louis when he wrote the first folk Mass setting in 1964. This Mass For Young Americans gained underground popularity for two years before it was recorded and published. Repp described his feelings when it was first used in a community Mass at the seminary: "My reaction," he said, "was like the one you hear about —'You mean a guitar in church?'" Repp later composed another setting and some very simple hymns which became widely known.

- John Ylvisaker, a Lutheran seminarian, began composing hymns in a style of the British balladeer. He sang the songs with an intimate, soft voice which was a contrast to the amplified sound of the rock musicians. Sometimes bordering on the story-teller's style, John wove imaginative lyrics through the images of Scripture. He edited a couple of hymnals for the Lutherans and received national attention with his Mass For The Secular City, performed and recorded at Carnegie Hall in 1967.

- Sydney Carter, an English poet-singer, is one of the best writers of texts in the folk idiom. He is well known for "Lord of the Dance" which was set to an old Shaker tune. He has composed many other works which are now published by Galliard in England.

- Reverend Richard Avery and Don Marsh, minister and choir director, respectively, began writing songs for their Presbyterian church in Port Jervis, New York. The music is of a style of the Broadway show-tune and the lyrics are imaginative and usually humorous. Don Marsh says that their ministry is one of "enlarging our vocabulary of gratitude." They've formed their own publishing company called Proclamation Productions, 7 Kingston Avenue, Port Jervis, New York 12771.

- Pete Scholtes, a Catholic priest in Chicago, composed "They'll Know We Are Christians By Our Love" for an ecumenical meeting of a Protestant church and a Catholic church in 1965. He mimeographed the song that he had written for the event. The people sang it and said that it was "nice." The same kind of "nice" that they talked about when the cake was served after Mass. Pete wrote the notes backwards, putting the stems on the wrong side of the notes.

    "I couldn't read music," he said. "I never
      intended to compose, and, when I did, I never
      intended to form a youth choir. When I did,

I never thought of taking them on tour and
recording. People call me a reactionary because I wrote that song. Others call me a
prophet. I'm neither."

- The Medical Mission Sisters of Philadelphia recorded some
  new hymns for the church which Sr. Miriam Therese Winter
  composed. Their albums: <u>Joy Is Like The Rain</u>, <u>I Know The
  Secret</u> and <u>Knock, Knock</u> have met with good commercial
  reception and are easily sung.

FOLK SONG SATURATION

In 1966, religious publishers began to churn out the music and
recordings to enable the churches to sing Folk Masses. The
demand for new music was there and the opportunity to cash in
on the need was there, also. New companies were initiated solely
for the need of new folk music, primarily in the Catholic churches,
and, then, later for the Protestant denominations. A few companies determined the directions and standards of the music.

As church folk music became big business, greater demand for
more music was made upon the composers. Unfortunately, many
of them who achieved notice quickly, did so on the basis of their
first works. The increased demands seemed to drain the amateur
composers of the creating spirit. Their later works sounded more
labored than spirited. As the Folk Masses became mass-produced,
churches started turning away from a dependency on the publishers
and started inviting the creativity of the local congregation.
The songs that arose within the parish were a wide spectrum of
quality, as you would expect. Those that were honest and easily
sung became pages of the local church's hymnody. It was during
this period of the late '60's that individual churches also wanted
to assert their autonomy from the publisher's rule by printing and
binding their own "loose-leaf" hymnals.

A FOLK FOOTNOTE

The Folk Mass and hymns in the church during the 1960's were not a
revolution, but an evolution. We all learned to live together a
little bit better because of the evolving spirit that the music
gave us. Some thought that the guitar would replace the organ as
<u>the</u> instrument in worship. Some thought that the casual and in-
formal style of the folk music would replace the more directed
style of the choral works. Neither situation happened. We

learned that no one instrument is holier than another instrument, nor was salvation of hymn singing going to come on the strings of a guitar alone. We learned that the formalized dignity could often be ritualized imprisonment of what worship should be. And, we experienced that forced joy or self-conscious casualness was no better.

Folk Masses may have been developed as a means of attracting the youth back into the church. As we soon found out, the music not only brought the youth, it also brought their parents who could appreciate the spirit and enthusiasm of the sound. People witnessed young people getting excited about worship, in a creative way.

Folk music's greatest appeal was also its most serious drawback. It is easily learned and does not require a great deal of musicianship to strum the simple chords. The Folk Masses became an expedient way of bringing new music into worship. The idiom was not too harsh to listen to or too demanding to play. These were qualities that soon would make "singing the same music again and again" as dulling as the church music we were seeking to up-date.

> Everytime you play, you've got to remember that it's a new time and a new day. You've got to sound that sense of wonder and excitement, the freshness and aliveness that is in you. You can't play the same music twice. It's just not you.

JAZZ AS SPIRITUAL EXPRESSION

> "Everybody has the blues. Everybody yearns for
> meaningful existence. Everybody wants to love
> and be loved. Everybody likes to clap hands
> and be happy. Everybody longs for faith. In
> music, and especially in that over-arching-
> category referred to as jazz, we are blessed
> with a means whereby all can be attained."
>
> Martin Luther King, Jr.
> Preface to Blues and Trouble

From the blues and the gospel songs of the church came the seeds
of jazz in the 20th century. It was no accident that the music
of the Afro-American community grew at a time when the "Negro"
was most isolated from the rights of full citizenship in America.
There is no way to stop the creative urge to express what's going on inside.

In the 1960's, in a time of cultural conformity, jazz was a
musical voice of freedom. It's improvisational style and
rhythmic complexities spoke of freedom's drive to realization.
It is no wonder that more and more artists were utilizing the
religious roots of jazz to speak to the nation's spirit as a
people moved towards freedom.

Jazz musicians, who for years had played music and recorded
for commercial recognition or the artistic recognition of
their peers, now devoted entire albums to spiritual music.

- During the summer of 1964, Randy Weston, pianist-
  composer, drew enthusiastic response when he led his
  quintet in a special jazz worship service, The Bible
  Speaks To You In Word And Music, at Judson Memorial
  Church in Greenwich Village. He did other performances of works which were Biblically inspired in
  connection with his work in civil rights, according
  to EBONY Magazine (1966: "Jazz Goes To Church").

- In December, 1964, John Coltrane, saxophonist, recorded
  LOVE SUPREME (Impulse AS-77) in gratitude to God "to
  whom all praise is due."

- Paul Horn, saxophonist-flutist urged Hollywood composer,
  Lalo Schifrin, to write a Jazz Suite On The Mass Texts
  (RCA LSP-3414). TIME Magazine (July 9, 1965) reported
  that Schifrin composed the suite "out of conviction that
  the vitality of jazz is the best way to modernize the
  spirit of church worship." Father Norman J. O'Connor

said that Schifrin is not the first to try composing for the Mass, nor is he the last. "But, what he has done at a moment in our lives when music is finding a new life in the church, is to turn our eyes from the past — where they have lingered much too long — to the present and to the future." The Suite is a concert work performed by a large instrumental ensemble with chorus.

- In May, 1965, pianist Vince Guaraldi (who popularized the Charlie Brown television shows with his trio work) recorded Vince Guaraldi at Grace Cathedral (Fantasy 3367), a modern setting for the choral Eucharist. He took Anglican plain-chant and set his trio behind the melodies.

- On June 19, 1965, Ed Summerlin premiered a new Liturgy of the Holy Spirit (Avante Garde Records) at the New York Conference of the Methodist Church. The work, with words by author, William Robert Miller, is based upon Hippolytus' 2nd century liturgy. It is written for vocal quartet, choir, congregation, minister and jazz ensemble. The text draws upon such worship forms as the agape and the epiklesis and uses "images and symbols which have not become clichés, which are not too debatable and which have durability, both theologically and metaphorically, as poetry."

- On September 16, 1965, Duke Ellington presented the first Concert of Sacred Music (RCA LPM 3582) at Grace Cathedral in San Francisco. With his big band, singers and a chorus, he led a packed house in what a critic called a "wondrous prayer." Ellington commented that: "Every man prays in his own language and there is no language that God does not understand."

  EBONY Magazine noted that: "Duke Ellington's recent sacred concerts have, perhaps, done the most to attract the public to a trend that has cut across racial and national boundaries."

- On January 26, 1966, the Dukes of Kent and I offered the first jazz service with the United Church of Christ denomination. The service featured an eight-piece band and a "word jazz" sermon created by Rev. Paul Stiffler.

- In 1966, Mary Lou Williams performed some of her religious compositions at Carnegie Hall. This event is recorded: Praise The Lord In Many Voices (Avante Garde Records), Volume II.

- Joe Masters recorded The Jazz Mass (Columbia CS 9398) for choir and jazz ensemble. This is a very usable piece for the local church, especially The Credo.

- On May 8, 1966, Eddie Bonnemere premiered <u>Missa Hodierna</u>
  in New York City. <u>AMERICA</u> (October 15, 1966) reported that
  the Mass, which uses the Latin text, is an immensely moving
  work and has been listed as one of the jazz events of the
  year, for it "most skillfully and reverently integrates"
  several modern styles into the liturgy.

- In 1967, Eddie Bonnemere composed <u>Mass For The Advent Season</u>
  for St. Thomas the Apostle church in Harlem. He also composed Masses for the seasons of Christmas and Easter and the
  <u>Mass For Every Season</u> for the period between Pentecost and
  Advent.

  > "Church music has to be natural, in the idioms of
  > our times, if people are really going to express
  > themselves in it. It has to be in a style they
  > feel personally, if they're going to be genuinely
  > involved in it. It can't be in some medieval
  > form out of another century, as it often is. It
  > should be in terms of people today."

- Chicago's Night Pastor, Bob Owens, and Seven Friends recorded <u>Chicago Jazz</u> (The Night Pastor, 30 East Oak, Chicago,
  Illinois 60611) as a means of adding financial support to
  the night ministry. The recording included a setting of
  Psalm 150 to "When The Saints Come Marching In" (1967).

- Ira Sullivan, a multi-instrumentalist, working in Florida
  in 1967, began working with local ministers in playing
  jazz in churches.

- In December, 1967, John Gensel of New York, recorded
  <u>O Sing To The Lord A New Song</u> (Fortress Press) with The
  Joe Newman Quintet. The musicians improvised around
  Psalm readings.

- On January 19, 1968, Duke Ellington presented the <u>Second
  Concert of Sacred Music</u> at St. John the Divine in New York.
  "I think of myself as a messenger boy," he wrote in the
  program notes, "one who tries to bring messages to people
  .... It has been said that what we do is to deliver lyri-
  cal sermons..."

- On February 2, 1968, Chicago newspapers reported: "Jazz
  Is Played To Open New British Church." The story told of
  how Princess Margaret, in mink coat and a high-crowned
  mink hat, joined in singing jazz hymns at the consecration
  of London's newest church in Old Southwark. "I had not
  been warned in advance, but I thought it was splendid,"

she said. The Bishop, Dr. Mervyn Stockwood, told the congregation, "I hope it won't be long before you get rid of some of the music you now have and use some of what you have heard today. I welcome the energy and vigor, the gaiety and dignity that is taking place today."

- In November, 1968, the Dukes of Kent and I developed a celebration in the jazz idiom which was premiered at Orchestra Hall in Chicago as a part of the Church Federation's Annual Youth Night. The event featured a sextet with scat choir and hymns for the congregation; one of which was "The Church Within Us." The music was later recorded on Celebration For Modern Man (Center For Contemporary Celebration).

- March 17, 1969, Eddie Bonnemere premiered Missa Laetare at New York's St. Peter's Church. This was a Lutheran Mass recorded by Fortress Press. Bonnermere said, "There are many languages in heaven and if jazz can speak to a man in need, God can use jazz to speak to him." Eddie began writing liturgical music because he felt that the formalistic rituals of the church weren't speaking to people in terms they understood.

While there are many other expressions of worship in the jazz idiom during this period, the ones that I have listed are significant because the majority of them are still available to you on record. It's interesting that some of the religious jazz was never performed in a church, but only in a recording studio (Coltrane, Horn); some jazz was recorded as a "document" of a live service or concert (Ellington); some was recorded in a studio after it has been experienced in a communal setting (Summerlin, Schneider, Bonnemere). Few of these jazz recordings were published by religious companies. And, unlike the folk composers of church music, most of the jazz composers were people who wrote from a position outside of the professional churchman. This fact would account for both the honesty in which the musician approached the writing of the music, and, sometimes, it accounted for the lack of integration which the music had in the liturgy. For me, the ideal composer of new music for the church is one who is both professional minister and musician, with the sensitivity of the artist and the sense of serving God.

EXPANDING RELIGIOUS EXPRESSION:
1967 - 1976

The liturgical mood was shifting near the end of the decade. No longer was the sermon the central event. It was now the whole liturgy and the whole participation of priest and congregation. There was an eagerness for unity — young and old, black and white. We realized that to keep distant from one another would be damaging to the dream that many people held.

Music during this time began to break through the barriers that had separated jazz, rock, folk, country and the classics. We heard jazz-rock or folk-rock, country-folk and jazz-rock-classical. This was a time of fusion.

> "I prefer not to be called a jazz musician or rock musician. Same with my music. I dislike categories and labels; they restrict you. I want my music to 'touch' people — to make them sad, happy, etc."
>
> John Klemmer, saxophonist
> All The Children Cried (Cadet - 326)

Often, finding the worship structure too confining, musicians began searching for alternative vehicles for expressing their spiritual growings. They worked with extended musical forms, such as the oratorio, cantata or the art-style called a "happening" in which various forms of media were combined into the whole. Some musicians began exploring Eastern religious music as a result of the influence of Indian musicians like Ravi Shanker.

- In July, 1967, Carla Bley's A Genuine Tong Funeral (RCA LSP 3988) was recorded by vibist Gary Burton, his quartet and orchestra. The liner notes state that: "This is a dramatic musical production based on emotions towards death." It is meant to be performed on a stage, with lights and costumes. The epilogue which closes the album is entitled "A Beginning" and features "The New National Anthem - Son of Jazz".....life goes on, back into the fray.

- In August 1967, Ed Summerlin worked with the rock group, Rotary Connection, to bring off a celebration of the Mass at the Liturgical Conference in Milwaukee. This involved dancers, musicians and multi-media. "I have become convinced," Ed wrote, "that we must do more action together in church services and make more use of projections and mixed media." He would later compose "Christ Lag in

Todesbanden: or Where Do We Go From Here?" for brass, strings, chorus and jazz trio, and "Sourdough and Sweetbread" for chorus, brass, jazz trio, eight projectors and three actors. These compositions are available on a rental basis from the composer.

- During September, 1967, Paul Horn recorded Cosmic Consciousness (World Pacific - 1445) as an expression of his new-found appreciation for the transcendental work of Maharishi Mahesh Yogi, the guru who influenced the Beatles' George Harrison. With the awareness of the global village, there was going to be no limit to the spiritual expression of the creative musician.

- On February 29, 1968, Dave Brubeck premiered his oratorio on the teachings of Jesus, Light In The Wilderness. He began composing the work in 1966 as an expression of his feeling over the sudden death of his 17-year-old nephew. The liberetto is drawn verbatim from the teachings of Jesus, and reveals the constant struggle of good and evil in the world. The premiere was performed by the Cincinnati Symphony and the Miami University Singers with an Ecumenical choir from 73 local churches.

- During 1968, Hair, a cultural celebration of the young, broke onto the Broadway stage. While not a religious work, it is significant as an expression of the times and the dreams people had. The opening theme of "Aquarius" is called a rock hymn in which the tribe mystically calls forth its vision of harmony and understanding. Hair (RCA LSO - 1150) would set a style for later expressions of Superstar, Godspell and Bernstein's MASS. Religious expression would become so integrated into cultural times (Jesus People, Billy Graham at the White House) that Broadway would become a dramatic stage for these rock "operas" built on the Jesus theme.

- On October 5, 1969, The Center For Contemporary Celebration created the first of a series of multi-media religious events at the University Church of Disciples, near the University of Chicago. This first one was "The World Is Dying For Love" and built upon the images of Genesis with creation and the fall. Actors, projectionists, a 9-piece jazz-rock ensemble and dancers were brought together, along with a congregation of over 500 people. It was shared on the evening of World Communion Sunday.

- On January 27, 1970, Oscar Brown Jr.'s <u>JOY</u> (RCA LSO - 1166) opened at the New Theatre in New York. <u>JOY</u> is described as a musical statement of the times "to raise hope, to entertain thoughts of jubilation and lamentations, with an emphasis on the time of joy."

- During Holy Week, 1970, The Center presented <u>"The Dream Died Lives</u>" — a Good Friday expression of the betrayal, the subtle crucifixion of people and the resurrection hope. We built upon the still too fresh sense of frustration about the killings of Dr. King, Robert Kennedy and the students at Kent State and Jackson State. A film was made of carrying a 100-pound telephone pole along Michigan Avenue. People of all ages would come and help carry the pole. We were curious to know what meaning a cross-like shape would have for people outside of the church. Choirs, multi-media, drama and a jazz-rock ensemble presented the work.

- On June 8, 1970, I was ordained to a ministry of celebration. I rented the Museum of Contemporary Art in Chicago, and, with an 8-piece band, dancers, a jazz choir and multi-media projections, a close community of people shared in the co-missioning of this ministry to the churches through the arts.

- On November 8, 1970, Alice Coltrane, jazz harpist, recorded <u>Journey In Satchidananda</u>(Impulse 9203), along with six other musicians, as her expression in meeting "my own beloved spiritual perceptor, Swami Satchidananda ....the first example I have seen in recent years of Universal Love of God in action."

- During this same period, two rock stars were getting into Eastern thought, Carlos Santana and Mahavishnu John McLaughlin. Together they recorded <u>Love Devotion Surrender</u> (Columbia KC 32034) as a means of promoting their spiritual guide, Sri Chinmoy.

- During Holy Week, 1971, The Center developed another Good Friday celebration, <u>"The Nail Is A Simple Machine</u>." During this Holy Week, Mayor Daley was being re-elected to his office and so the awareness of a machine in politics would be prominent with the Chicago community. "The Nail" explored the possibility that Pilate was just a cog in the political machine of his day. Nails were distributed to everyone and a meditation was shared at the beginning of the service. Media, music in a jazz-rock style and choirs were featured.

- In March, 1973, we premiered The Sonrise Of Imagination, a concert of religious music that I had been composing during the past two years. I formed a new band called Inner Peace, a 9-member jazz-rock ensemble. With a 30-voice choir, dancers and media, concerts were presented in Chicago, Indianapolis and Detroit.

- On October 24, 1973, Duke Ellington presented his Third Sacred Concert To The Majesty Of God (RCA APL 1-0785) at Westiminster Abbey. This would be the last concert for the composer, for Ellington would soon be facing the majesty of God.

- On Good Friday, in 1974 and 1975, The Center presented "Into Your Hands". It was a drama-musical-multi-media expression of the disciples who followed and deserted Jesus during the events of Holy Week. The work called for actors to take the roles of Jesus and the Disciples, the role of Pilate and Simon, the tavern owner. A choir, with an 8-piece band, was used along with multi-media (three projectors, two overheads) and dancers.

- In February, 1975, I composed The Mass For New Beginnings, a jazz setting for choir, congregation and instrumental quintet. This was premiered at a Sunday night midnight Mass at St. Thomas Aquinas Center at Purdue University. After every Mass, it is customary for the students to fill out a liturgy questionnaire giving their reactions to the service, music, sermon, etc. About 90 per cent of the students were very enthusiastic about the setting. "We should do this all the time," was typical of their responses. About 10 per cent thought that the Mass was too jarring and upsetting. "It was a 'show'. Let's go back to the old way — the Folk Mass." One of the priests shared a Liturgical Questionnaire that had been taken nine years earlier when the first English Mass in a folk style was introduced. About 90 per cent thought that it was great and 10 per cent wanted to go back to the "old way" — the Latin Mass with the organ. I wonder what the questionnaire ten years from now will be about and what will be the "old way" in 1985?

- On January, 25, 1976, Rev. Paul Stiffler and I celebrated our tenth year since the first jazz service in the United Church of Christ. We had a workshop in new church music, a concert of some of my recent writings and a liturgy on

Sunday. Paul's sermon, from that service, appears later in the book in the section "The Creative Minister At Worship."

On March 6, 1976, <u>Come Share The Spirit,</u> a concert of my new religious works was presented in Indianapolis with choirs from DePauw University, a 9-piece jazz-rock ensemble, Sr. Adelaide's multi-media and Dolores Layer, soloist.

WHERE HAVE ALL THE FLOWERS GONE?

The incidents at Kent State and Jackson State were deadening to the renewal in May of 1969. One last fling at the tribal meeting called "Woodstock" in August of that year was like a freeze-frame of the decade that had protested against war, marched for freedom, sang songs in the streets, coffee houses and churches. People had hoped in love, and, now, the guns, which had cut down many of the leaders, took the lives of the flowers as well. The real tragedy of the era was not that the people had failed to create the revolution of love, but that they thought they had achieved it.

The hope of renewing the liturgy, new music and creative religious expression was shattered by the end of the '60's. Renewal had come to mean hectic, random experimentation —liturgies of the absurd were being substituted for the religious melodrama. "Celebration" had become a slogan, a bandwagon that every church had to get on at least once. Churches searched for a "group-ness" in worship that was too often accompanied by gimmicks, carnival music, balloons, rhetoric ("Today is the first day of the rest of your life" or "Celebrate Life!") and a nebulous doctrine that the "contemporary" was somehow different that the "traditional."

Ralph Thibodeau's article "Threnody For Sacred Music, 1968" (COM-MONWEAL, December 13, 1968) summed up the feelings that were prevalent near the end of the decade:

> "The inescapable fact is that the 'People of God'
> have been had. Either they listen to the drivel
> that passes for congregational participation at
> the normal parish Mass, or they go with the kids
> to the Hootenanny Mass to have their ears assaulted
> and their minds insulted."

Churches began wondering "where has all this taken us? What have we gained?" By 1970, there was a noticeable pulling back from anything that sounded "experimental." The emphasis that had been placed on worship earlier in the decade by major denominations began to diminish. Those who had occupied offices of worship in some denominational headquarters either resigned or were released due to economic pressures. Their positions were not filled. The responsibilities for developing creative worship were given to another already over-loaded department.

What happened to the people who were involved in the years of freedom and ferment? What happened to the musicians who were working in the folk, jazz and rock idioms in the church?

Many became discouraged and disillusioned, not only by the government and what was happening in the culture, but also by the church which too often acted only when it was "safe." Some left the organized ministry to minister in God's name in other ways. The majority of people, that I know, went "underground," working within the communities, enabling the creativity of the local churches to once again find their roots and begin building and growing. Some went to work in a personal way, with the people. Today, we are beginning to see some of the fruits of those who have labored over the years to keep the spirit of freedom and honesty alive in the church and its worship.

A NEW AWARENESS

Since 1969, my work at The Center For Contemporary Celebration has taken me into local churches throughout the United States and Canada. I've lived and struggled with people who were hungry for new ideas in worship and for music that had content and meaning. I've created with people who needed to write their own hymns and to design the liturgies for their people. I've prayed with people who were confused and frustrated about what was going on in the churches. I've celebrated both the joy and the sorrow of daily life with large and small groups. In every situation, people were urgent about expressing what was inside them. They were searching for the roots that they could tap to affirm their faith in a way that had meaning. The decade of the '60's taught us that effective worship must be expressive worship. No longer would the people be content to sit through no-content services. If worship is to be significant, it must be filled with meaning that we can take seriously and joyously.

We had learned a lot from the period of freedom and ferment:

- people can exist in creative tension and still love one another. To worship doesn't mean we all have to be doing the same thing at the same time. There's room for the creativity of the congregation as well as the minister's and the musician's.

- we search for our commonality — not for our differences.

- out of tension can come a strengthened unity. Worship may take many forms and styles, yet its function is the same. When the folk, rock and jazz music entered the church in the '60's, they were seen as alien forms of religious music. However, as adults listened to the young people and as the youth heard the older generation, the "gap" began to be bridged. We all learned that being young or being old was not a reason for making battle. We needed to work together in order to survive.

- recognizing our distinctiveness, both physically and culturally, increased our sensitivity to personal needs. We had become sensitized to feelings, to other people's traditions, to the contributions that other races made, to the society and to the spirit that various kinds of celebration brought to our whole community. This growing appreciation and respect for the traditions of others made us more open in a time when many doors were being closed.

- recognizing the need for spiritual development whether it was through jazz, folk, rock, the classics; transcendental meditation, Eastern or Western mysticism, Zen; physical disciple, or Yoga, people of all ages began searching for inner peace in a time when the outer peace was decidedly temporary. People felt the need for mystery, wonder and awe.

- integrating the music and the liturgical action became significant. No longer could we simply stick in three or four hymns and expect instant worship with meaning. We learned that new music often demands a new framework for the liturgy. Formula worship patterns were not the answer. The music caused us to re-think what worship was all about.

- experimentation and innovation are always necessary, but such work must be done with integrity and thought as to the meaning that a new hymn, liturgical text or action will have for the life of the congregation.

- music for the church is not to be judged on whether it is old or new, it is simply good or bad music. For a while, we based our judgment of a musical piece on whether it was "contemporary." Congregations soon found that some of the "contemporary" hymns were as meaningless as some of the 19th century hymns. The '60's were a formative time for the hymns of the church. From this decade, a few songs have emerged that will become standards in Christian hymnody, a phenomenon which has occurred throughout the history of church music.

CHURCH MUSIC IN THE PRESENT TENSE

For the music of the church today, we can neither afford an exclusive commitment to the past nor a limited philosophy that permits an "anything goes" style of liturgics and music. We must seek the best of both the traditional and the contemporary resources, always remembering that music is either good or bad. It should not be judged on whether it's new or old.

Here are some probes that I've used in evaluating church music:

Does the music fit the liturgy?

> No matter how outstanding the musical piece may be, if it doesn't fit the flow of the service, then it is an obstacle rather than a transparent pathway to God.

Does the music fit the people?

> If liturgy is to be an expression of the people, then the music must also express the faith in styles that hold meaning for the community. To use music as "shock treatment" or a polite form of punishment is not what the music of the church is about.

Do the texts fit the music?

> While we were once quick to pit the new against the old, today we are all too quick to weld the two together without considering how they fit. Many texts still speak in country imagery - sheep, seraphim, hills, mountains — a rural faith. Are the words really meaningful to the people? Are they rooted in a common experience? For me, one of the most glaring incompatibilities of text and song is the combination of The Doxology with Hernando's Hideaway.

Is there an artistic integrity to the music?

> To what degree is an enthusiasm being communicated in the way the music is played or sung? Does the sound feel like it is being freshly created for this particular time or does it sound like it's a repeated commodity?

We have passed through the patronizing stages of liturgical music when styles such as folk, jazz or rock were thought of as a means of getting the kids into church. We've learned that worship is an action of the entire body and not just segments of it. This, however, should not lead the church musician to put together a liturgical smorgasbord of various styles of music in the hope of pleasing everyone. Such consideration has usually led to more confusion that inspiration. Whatever we do, should be done in a style that brings a wholeness to the religious event.

The church musician will need to develop a knowledge of chanting (both Western and Eastern) polyphonic music, chorale hymns, the psalms of Gelineau, the spirit of Black music in the church, folk hymns and jazz stylings.

The church musician will also need to become composer as well as per-sonal former. To feel that you, as a musician, are incapable of making some personal statement through your original sounds, is to limit your own possibilities. To feel that the church doesn't need your originality, is to overlook the possibilities within the church. The creative church musician today must seek originality and integrity, to bring both the past and the present into a meaningful relationship in the midst of the worshipping community.

A JAZZ TAG ON THIS SET

So far we've looked at the climate of the late '50's and early '60's, the folk scene and the jazz scene in the church. Unlike the Folk Mass market, jazz was not as reproducable for the local congregation. There were no church jazz publishers that were flooding the market with available charts. Instrumental jazz was not a typical vehicle of expression for the young person in a guitar and rock dominated culture. However, today's young musician has the opportunity in high school and college to become more proficient in jazz and improvising through educational courses. There is, in 1976, a growing talent resource of young instrumental musicians who could be available to the church in playing jazz music.

The Center For Contemporary Celebration has begun publishing religious jazz arrangements designed for choirs, congregations and instrumental ensembles. These are starting to be used by college communities and churches which have access to school jazz programs. There is a new spirit coming on.

Jazz is a personal expression. You reveal a great deal about yourself when you play it. For this reason, jazz is a tremendous vehicle for spiritual expression. The danger in this music is that, for worship purposes, when the music needs to have a corporate dimension as well as a personal one, that the jazz will become so personalized that nobody else can share in the meaning. The jazz style can also become so identified with its creator that it would be hard for another musician to play it. For example, it's hard for me to conceive of another band playing Duke Ellington's Concert of Sacred Music without Duke Ellington. The question is: "Can you take another jazz musician's music and make it your own?" Of course you can! The way you do it is to add yourself in improvisational ideas.

Jazz is not an individualistic music. It is corporate by nature. You can't play jazz alone. It requires someone to hear it as well as someone to play with it. Primarily, in order for jazz to be authentic, it demands the expressive risk of the person who makes it.

> "Everytime God's children have thrown away fear
> in pursuit of honesty — trying to communicate —
> understood or not — miracles have happened."
>
> Duke Ellington
> Program Notes, Concert of Sacred Music
> September 16, 1965

FURTHER READING

APPRECIATING INDIA'S MUSIC, Emmons E. White. India: Wesley
   Press, 1957.

GREAT MUSICIANS OF INDIA, Dolly Rizvi. Bombay: IBH Publishing
   Company, 1968.

LOUIS, Max Jones and John Chilton. Boston: Little, Brown and
   Company, 1971.

THE MAKING OF A COUNTER CULTURE, Theodore Roszak. New York:
   Doubleday and Company, Inc., 1969.

THE NEW EDITION OF THE ENCYCLOPEDIA OF JAZZ, Leonard Feather.
   New York: Crown Publishers, Inc., 1960.

ROCK ENCYCLOPEDIA, Lillian Roxon. New York: Workman Publishing Company, 1969.

THE SUFI MESSAGE OF HAZRAT INAYAT KHAN, VOL. 2. London:
   Barrie Books, Ltd., 1962.

YOUNG PEOPLE AND THEIR CULTURE, Ross Snyder. Nashville:
   Abingdon Press, 1969.

VIBRATIONS, David Amram. New York: Macmillian Company, 1968.

WE CALLED IT MUSIC, Eddie Condon. New York: Henry Holt and
   Company, 1957.

THE WORLD OF POP MUSIC AND JAZZ, William Robert Miller.
   St. Louis: Concordia Publishing House, 1965.

PART THREE

DESIGNING LITURGY:

A Musician's View

DESIGNING LITURGY:
A Musician's View

In planning a worship event, the musician often feels inadequate because of a lack of theological education when compared to that of the minister's. But, the musician needs to remember that he or she brings skills and resources to preparing for worship that the average minister does not have. The creative musician needs to draw upon those musical resources and artistic sensitivities that are uniquely the musician's. It is essential, however, that the minister and musician function together and not as two separate specialists. This section looks at the art of designing liturgy from the musician's point of view. I first discuss some important understandings of the liturgical options that can be used. Then I share a worship design which began with music. I think this will be useful since often the musician prepares some special piece or invites guest musicians to play the work, and, unless the service picks up on the piece, both the service and the music will seem out of joint.

Liturgy — the communal expression of a people.

Liturgy is done by a people. It is not a formula or a repeatable pattern into which we can plug readings or hymns.

Liturgy is a people's art form, a way of sharing a corporate faith. It is not the work of just one minister. It is an expression of a whole family of God. Those who would prepare for worship, do so on behalf of the whole community. For this reason, it is essential that those designing liturgy be in touch with the needs of the people.

Liturgy is a time of commitment when people come together, not because they have to, but because they want to. They are nourished by what goes on, rather than bored. You see, worship should not be something we have to endure. God doesn't want us to suffer in our religion. Christianity calls us to life, not to death.

Liturgy is an action of faith expressed through song, dance, drama, light, speaking words, historic and contemporary accounts of people who have lived in the midst of God's Presence.

> Some people try to distinguish between 'tradition' and 'contemporary.' I can't, because for me, they are one in the same. The 'tradition' is that movement through history that has kept us going and brought us to this point in life. The 'contemporary'

is what we, as a people who identify with a 'tradition,' choose to risk to keep that tradition alive and moving on to the next generation. Without that risking, the 'tradition' becomes lifeless and merely a commemorative repetition.

Liturgy is a living tradition rather than a recitation of the past by a people enslaved to a printed bulletin.

Effective liturgy will be an embodiment of the qualities and meanings of those who gather. It will be expressive, rather than repressive, of the beliefs which are that people. There will be freedom, times of spontaneity, joy and sorrow, re-living and re-forming a particular style of life in the world called Christian.

Liturgy (meaning "work of the people") may take various styles:

Recovery - In the mid-19th and later in the 20th centuries, when historians probed the early Christian church, there were uncovered numerous forms of liturgical practice. "The earlier, the better" seemed to be the standard of excellence and acceptability. This historical research made churches aware of various creeds, worship practices and historical situations of the Judeo-Christians. While having many benefits of getting us in touch with our roots, this approach also unearthed many liturgical oddities that were terribly "out of time" with the present. This practice was as gimmicky as any other, when it did not authentically express the needs of the people.

Renewal - Gaining impetus from Vatican II in the early '60's, renewal sought to bring meaning out of familiar forms already in use. Most of the new music of the period would be characterized by this term, since it rarely caused the liturgy to be re-shaped. It merely fit into the already existing spots. Renewal did not seek to throw out the old, but was willing to continue with the familiar, but from a new perspective.

Re-shaping - This style is still in its infancy for we are only able to grasp its future meaning at certain times. Re-shaping the liturgy for each occasion when the faithful gather is becoming increasingly a greater option, because the church has been unable to re-establish its roots in the tradition of the past, or to interpret the present situation of life with any real significance. In spite of the talk of renewal, little has actually happened to transform the gathering of the Christian community. Too often, renewal efforts have become denominational slogans or cultural bandwagons which are easily dissipated. However, re-shaping will be carried on by a small group of committed people scattered throughout the country. These groups have been at work and developing, largely without much media attention, since 1968.

Re-shaping the liturgy will be characterized by a constant re-examination of culture, the meaning and need for ritual, the necessity of creative expression and the possibilities of people together. Re-shaping will remain alive, perpetuated by creative-doubt encountering faith, through which all "givens" will be questioned and appropriated if they have meaning.

Re-shaping the liturgy is rooted in the tradition and seeks to apply the meaning of that tradition to the present. This style of liturgy will not be limited to any one place. It will be interwoven with the common experience of the people, who are willing to suffer and endure, to rejoice and persist, in what they believe is right and just.

Re-shaping will establish precedents that the renewal movement may want to adapt five years later.

Effective liturgy is good composition.

Like a musical work, the liturgy will have a beginning, a middle and an end. It will have direction, a sense of movement towards a climax. There will be peaks and valleys, a sense of drama.

A thematic idea will be stated. There may be variations created on that theme, or the theme may need to be restated throughout the work. It is the same with the liturgy: we need to take one central idea that has importance for the life of the community and speak it significantly.

One of the major weaknesses in worship services is that we use a shot-gun approach, scattering out a variety of ideas through the readings, the sermon, choral anthems, pastoral prayers and hymns so that nothing comes through with intensity. The service becomes that smorgasbord event where so many different things are given that we never really develop any tastes. At the conclusion of such a service, the congregational member finds it difficult to remember just what it was that he or she digested.

Often, these kinds of services stay in a comfortable middle ground. There is little creative tension, a sensing of the

heights and depths, the hopes and despairs of the people.
Such services are dominated by the printed bulletin, which
is a convenient way to hide honest feelings.

It is also very important that the development of the central idea
be one that has grown out of the experience of the total life of
the community. It is not something invented by a few "planners"
of worship.

As the community works to give design to the liturgy, they search
out all the nuances of the central idea, and, like a good melody,
interweaves the parts together to form a journey with highs and
lows, conveying a historical thrust through time as well as a
depth dimension of our relation to God and to one another.

A major weakness in many worship services is that each part:

- prelude-hymn-call to worship;
- confession-pardon-faith statement;
- hymn-sermon-pastoral prayer;
- announcements-offering-doxology;
- hymn-recessional-benediction;

is separately developed, rather than thought of as parts of
a whole. The problem with this, is that you can never build up
any dramatic flow. The liturgy is always starting and stopping.
It never goes anywhere. We've blocked the service off into
chunks in which certain things go on at certain times. The service has become segmented. We need to develop ways of bringing
these parts into a total framework. Musically, this can be done
with simple transitions which I will share with you in the last
section of this chapter.

CHARTING THE LITURGY

CHART: a sheet giving information in a diagram
or table; an outline on which information can be plotted or written.

The Center For Contemporary Celebration has designed more than 300
different styles of liturgy for churches, colleges, penal institutions, for campers, religious educators, street gangs, youth groups,
high schools and hospitals. Not one service went just as we had
planned. There was always the unexpected innovation which emerged
from the people and became an important offering in the service.
But, this is what effective liturgy is all about — the work and
offerings of the people who gather.

In a service on the meaning of the Beatitudes, we
had read the scripture and discussed some of the
interpretation of the word 'blessed.' One interpretation was the word 'happy.' There were many
children present at worship that morning so I
asked one of the five-year-olds, "what is it like
to be HAPPY?" With a few moments of deep
thought, the child reared back his head and began to laugh. The whole congregation laughed
with him. That was a turning point from presentation to participation as the people began
internalizing the meaning of the Beatitudes. The
child's response couldn't have been planned for
or anticipated. It was that joyous risk of the
spontaneous.

So we learned that you cannot <u>plan</u> for celebration's spontaneity,
but you can <u>prepare</u> for it. It's much like making preparations
for a journey. You gather things that you anticipate you will
need. You plot your travel, realizing that your chart may be
subject to revision depending on the needs of the people with
whom you journey.

The idea of charting the liturgy is like mapping out new territory
to be explored. You will begin at a certain place and move with
all your resources, your knowledge of the terrain and your wealth
of experiences, to chart out a new land. To chart is not to
experiment in a random way. It is a continuing expansion of your
awareness of what it means to be in the world and in the midst of
God. The inroads and trail markings which your people have made
will be what you pass on to the next generation who will follow
your path and pioneer new trails.

In jazz, a 'chart' is a sheet of music from which the
band reads and improvises. To that chart, the musician
brings a knowledge of the instrument, resources and a
wealth of experience to play out new ideas. The chart
usually provides the thematic, rhythmic and harmonic
progressions of the music. It is within this framework
that the player expresses his or her own ideas and
freedom.

Similarly, in the liturgy, there are 'progressions'
around which the people build and move. The liturgy
provides a framework in which the people express their
prayers, faith and spirit. The liturgy is not an already established ordering into which we make things
fit. The ordering grows out of the meaning and the
experiences of the community. What we do is to prepare
pathways along which the people are free to move through
the liturgy.

Whenever we begin preparing for a celebration, we keep asking our-selves:

> Who are the people who are celebrating and what gifts, needs and resources do they bring?
>
> What are we celebrating? What is being proclaimed?
>
> How are the people going to participate? What meaning does this liturgy hold for them? When does presentation become participation?

Once the direction of the journey has been established, we then need to look at some of the elements that occur and will re-occur throughout every celebration:

GATHERING is the re-membering into a people.

The way we begin is crucial. An author noted that the first five minutes and the last five minutes of any meeting or conversation will tell you a great deal about the quality of that relationship. We can apply that also to the way we greet each other in worship. If the words are cold and formal, chances are, so is the community. If the music is somber as people gather, chances are that the style of the liturgy will be of the same tone.

The GATHERING must be a time of re-membering this people. It should re-awaken a communal awareness of God's Presence, the heritage and history-now-being-made in which we share. Rarely, if ever, do congregational readings/responses or "words of praise" adequately unite individuals, strangers and families into a People. The GATHERING needs to take in the fresh experiences and new mean-ings which this group has had since we were last together.

The GATHERING needs to be a fresh focusing of whose people we are each time we meet. It must be authentic and a style of prelude to what is coming. It should not be a repeatable commodity from week to week.

> So many times when people come to church they still carry with them some of the frustrations and experiences of the week or of that morning. They are hardly ready to settle in and worship. We need to help our people to <u>prepare</u> for the celebration.
>
> I've had some good results with two styles of preparation at the beginning of the communal celebration: one is

chanting a word like 'shalom' or 'om'; the other is inviting
the people to use their imagination in a guided meditation
such as:

> "Take a deep breath as we prepare to come together
> for worship this day. Take another breath and
> take in the life-giving oxygen of the environment
> and give back to the earth what you no longer need.
> Keep on breathing and feel yourself rise and fall
> inside as the air goes in and comes out. God has
> given you life. He breathed into mankind the
> breath of life. With your eyes closed, keep
> sensing that life in you as we listen to the life-
> giving sound of the prelude."

It is simply a way of taking time to prepare the people for
what they are about to experience so that when they hear
the music, they aren't just going to watch it being played.
They will be open to letting the music dwell inside them.

The tone of GATHERING is one of warmth and welcome, instead of
the cold cathedral chills. In some way, the people are made
aware that they are personally present to one another. Music
will set the tone of the GATHERING.

PROCLAIMING is the event of God-with-us.

No matter what form our proclamation takes (sermon, film, dance,
anthem, hymn, scripture), it should have the quality of "event."
The Hebrew mind used the word "dabar" to mean that words became
something to experience, not just something to be read. When
the Hebrew invoked - "in the name of God" - he sensed the calling
of God's Presence into the very midst of the community. In our
styles of proclamation, we must strive for such a quality of
presence, as if the events of our heritage were understandably
unfolding before us.

> "I've been working with the use of solo instruments to
> interpret the readings of scripture. It seems to me
> that when we read 'Sing a new song to the Lord'
> (Psalm 98), and do not hear a new song sung, that
> we are missing the fullness of the event."

What we PROCLAIM must have an intensity and a focusing rather
than a weak diffusion of meaning. Our words would seek to
penetrate into the meaning of God's Presence in the midst of
the world and our daily experiences.

One of the most effective styles of PROCLAMATION for me
has been the kind of interweaving of scripture, preached
word and sung word, which ministers are doing more and
more. I don't mean the sterotyped style of commenting
on the latest hit record after the congregation has
heard it played on the church's record player. I'm
talking about the style in which the minister's words
are amplified by the musician's creativity or the choir's
resources. This kind of sermon is one of the most powerful I've heard. Part of its power comes from the fact
that many people are involved in the delivery. The
chapter on "The Creative Minister At Worship" presents
one such sermon style created by Rev. Paul Stiffler.

CONFESSING is admitting the Christ to one another.

We are dealing with the wholeness of a person when people gather
for worship. We are not dealing just with certain segments. We
deal with mind and intellect as well as feelings of hope and hurt.
The CONFESSING is the input of the ambiguous nature of all life
and human existence. It is both affirmation and realization that
life is neither totally bad nor totally good and that we are called
to decide and work with the real situation, which is often the
choice between evils.

CONFESSION is choosing.

> "Behold, I set before you this day, life and good,
> death and evil; therefore, choose life. Choose
> you this day whom you will serve."

CONFESSING is living with answerable courage for the choices we
have made. We confess the unconquerable "nevertheless" to prevalent stupidities, ambiguities, to comfort and fashion. We choose
to live.

CONFESSING carries the incognition liturgy which we encounter every
day in the news and other media. It brings the awareness that
Christ is our brother, dying and rising each moment of the day.
We confess that our lives are interwoven and that when one person
suffers, the people suffer; and when one person is filled with
joy, we co-enjoy together.

CONFESSION must be both personal as well as communal. There must
be opportunity for the personal speaking as well as the community's

voicing. For me, printed confessions are not very effective for expressing either the personal or the communal feelings of the people. Too often the printed confession asks us to respond with words that are not real or authentic.

> "Father, Forgive Us" is a hymn from Come Share The Spirit. It is a prayer of confession seeking God's forgiveness for those things which we have not done, for times when we failed to extend ourselves to those in need. The second part of the song is one of thanksgiving for all that God has given us. During the hymn, there is a pause for the choir to hum and the minister to lead the congregation in a time of prayer. Not only do we sing about prayer, we also do it, but in such a way as to interweave the prayer into the hymn itself. To sing the confessional prayer has become a most effective liturgical style.

CONFESSION is an act of loving. It is the reconciliation of man with God through Jesus Christ. The PROCLAMATION comes as the separation of ourselves from God and from mankind, the world and ourselves is finally at an end. Our origin of unity with God is returned.

OFFERING is what we make, not something we take

In many churches, particularly within Protestant denominations, the OFFERING is that time in a service when the ushers take the people's money. The action has almost become habitual.

The OFFERING could be a most important action of the people, a time when we move out of the pews to a central place of giving, and make an OFFERING of ourselves, our gifts, our ideas, our music. This could be a time of giving more than money — a time of giving poems, new songs, dance. The choir might offer an anthem to prepare us for the giving.

> So often, music that is used with the offertory seems like it is purely background sound to diminish the noise of the coins in the metal plates. I've often used hymns which were sung as people made their offerings. If music was to be played, I would take time to introduce the music that would set the environment for the giving so that people understood that the music was not just a filler.

After the offering had been received, I would offer a
prayer or invite the community to offer the prayer.
When it is appropriate, the choir will offer a musical
prayer of thanksgiving. With the people gathered
around the altar, the minister says "let us pray...."
and the choir begins singing a song of thanksgiving.

The OFFERING can also be a time of commissioning a member of the
congregation to work on behalf of the community. For example,
one minister will take five dollars from each Sunday's offering
and give it to some member of the community to invest on behalf
of the community. Church members are then asked to report back,
in a few weeks, how they chose to invest that money in ministry
in the world. That simple action has heightened the congregation's
awareness of the offering.

OFFERING is a style of re-cycling — for we have been given much
by God. In receiving, we are also called to giving, to actualize
ourselves for the transformation of each day. We are called to
pour our days of living into God for transformation. We move to
the altar for alteration — to give ourselves to others in God's
service. We offer the work of our hands for upbuilding the
world and for passing it on to future generations. We realis-
tically share in the death and creation that is our world and
ourselves.

SCATTERING is the "Processional Benediction"

If "come, follow me" is one organizing image for the GATHERING,
then the commissioning to "go into all the world" is what organizes
our moving out. Our time of celebration does not cease when we
leave each other — it continues, but in different ways and in a
multitude of places and with many people.

With the SCATTERING we move from a time of renewing strength of
the community to a renewing of our personal vocation in the world.
Because we have been together, we can bounce back from disaster
and defeat.

Instead of always using speaking words as the benediction,
I will teach the people a short chant which sums up what
we've been about during the day. This style of a sung
benediction is then carried out into the streets. It's
a thrilling experience to be moving with a singing people
as we leave the building.

The following is one example of a benediction chant. It appears in the hymnal COME SHARE THE SPIRIT.

ONLY IN THE MIDST OF THE WORLD

Kent Schneider

BUILDING A SERVICE AROUND MUSIC

The Center was asked to design a Lenten service for a university community. The campus minister asked the staff to come and work with the students in preparing a special service. We would have access to a fine choir, instrumental musicians from the jazz program, some dancers and students from the religion and art departments.

I had just completed two new pieces that I thought would be of use in the service. One was based on Psalm 51: "Create in me, O Lord, a clean heart and put a new and right Spirit in me." The other was a hymn in the jazz idiom, entitled "Lord Inspire Our Worship." Beyond these two compositions, the structure of the service was wide open.

I began planning by asking: "What does 'create in me' mean for this university community?" I wondered how a college-aged person would express the Psalmist's prayer to "create a new Spirit in me." I discussed this with the staff and with some of the students who would be involved in the event. They shared recent experiences of sensing God's creating Spirit within their lives.

With this living documentation from the students and staff, I
thought:

- God is constantly offering us the opportunity to share in
  the creating action going on in the world. (PROCLAMATION)

- Each person has the freedom to participate in the creating
  or the destruction of life. (CONFESSION)

- God has shown us how we could live in the world through
  Jesus the Christ as we choose to pour ourselves out for
  the sake of others. (OFFERING)

In a very simple way, I had described one possible movement of the
liturgy for the service.

What could become a centering image for this event? What could be
a memorable symbol of God's invitation to share in creation?

> I remembered the meaning of Jeremiah 18 in which God
> is the potter who can build up or break down what he
> creates. When the creation gets out of hand, the
> potter smashes the work and starts again.

Clay could become a memorable image if it was set within a framework that gave it new meaning and took it out of the all too
familiar realm of play school activities. I checked with the art
department and made contact with the head of the ceramics and
pottery division who was very willing to work in the service. I
shared the idea of making the potter and the clay a centering
image in the event, and we decided that it could be very effective
if he simply sat in front of the altar throughout the service and
made pots.

I rehearsed the evening before the service with the choir and
musicians and I briefed them on what they needed to do in addition
to the music. They would be seated among the students in the
congregation and, after the prelude, would begin coming forward
from all parts of the church. The choir would not wear robes
and would be scattered throughout the church.

The dancers had never worked together before. Some of them were
more experienced than others. I had made a tape of the music
that they could dance to. I started working with them to give
some bodily shape to the prelude "Create In Me, O Lord." I'm
not a dancer, but I know what looks good and what looks terrible.
As a musician, I simply had the girls move out the feeling in
the music or the movement of the melody. I had learned that dance

will take place on various levels or energy planes. I was also
aware of what kind of movements were interesting and which ones
were lacking in energy. After a couple of hours, the dancers
were ready to put their movements to the musicians' instrumental
playing.

The Shape of the Service

Gathering

> (As students filled the sanctuary, the potter was already
> at work throwing clay on the wheel. He would do this
> throughout the service. Every student received a small
> chunk of clay which was wrapped in cellophane. The
> dancers were still rehearsing. The campus minister
> greeted the students and introduced me and the Center
> staff.)

> I shared with the students that in this period of Lent we
> would explore the Psalmist's prayer of 'create in me a
> clean heart and a new Spirit.' I invited them to share
> in the movement of the service as fully as they could.
> We rehearsed portions of the hymns, which were new to the
> group, and then we prepared to receive the prelude.

> "Create In Me, O Lord" with dancers, instrumentalists,
> vocalist.

> "Come Share The Spirit" from the hymnal by the same title,
> served as a calling to gather. The chant was taught to
> the whole congregation. As the song grew, the choir mem-
> bers, one by one, rose from the pews and came forward,
> forming a group on the altar stairs. They softened the
> chant as I spoke the following phrases, which the congre-
> gation repeated back:

> > We are God's People....
> > we are not alone....
> > we are interwoven, one with the other....
> >
> > when one is hurting....
> > we all share the sorrow....
> > when one is crying....
> > we all share the tears....
> >
> > We are God's People....
> > we are not alone....
> > we are interwoven, one with the other....

```
when one is caring....
the load's a bit lighter....
when one is sharing....
the day seems brighter....

We are God's People....
we are called to create....
to build....
to grow.....
to love.....
we are not alone....
we are interwoven, one with the other....
```

Amen.......**AMEN**....**AMEN !**

With choir, band and community, we finished "Come Share The Spirit" once more and moved into singing "Lord Inspire Our Worship."

Proclamation

The sermon was built upon the passage in Jeremiah and dealt with the need for the courage to create in an environment all too often dominated by technology and the "hardware" of life. The element of risk and revelation of the self in any creative acting was focused upon.

Confessing

This moved into a time of Confessing and prayer, which the community formed spontaneously. After each prayer, the musicians and choir responded with a short chant. The confessing took the shape of prayers when we had failed to act in a creative way, or when elements in the society acted in a destructive way. A prayer for the community was voiced by a campus leader and then there was a time of silence. Out of this silence came "Song of Love," a vocal and trumpet solo with tape accompaniment of a harpsichord played through an echoplex machine. A flute followed this, softly stating the melody line to "Amazing Grace" which was picked up by the band.

While the musicians were playing an arrangement of the song, I spoke words of hope that God has called us from destruction into the light of continued creation. Even

when we have failed, God's grace and love gives us hope
to go on. With that introduction, the whole community
sang Jim McBride's arrangement of "Amazing Grace" with
new words by Sister Adelaide.

Offering

This was a time of personalizing what each member of the
congregation could offer to continue God's creation. The
people were invited to take their piece of clay and to
shape it, like the potter did, as a sign of who they were
or as a sign of their hopes in the world. After about five
minutes of shaping, the community was invited to share the
meaning of their expression with another person.

From here, the pairs were asked to team up with two or
three other pairs by forming a hub of hands (placing one
hand in the middle of the circle of people and piling
hand on top of hand). The hubs of people were standing.
I invited them to go up as high as they could go, still
touching hands. Then I asked them to take the hub down
as low as they could go. I pointed out that people come
together when times are down or when times are up. We
rarely come together when life is in the comfortable
middle ground.

As a further deepening of the sharing, and still remaining
in the hub circles, the community was invited to take a
piece of the clay that they had shaped and to exchange it
with other people. In this way, even the clay symbol was
transformed by the interweaving of many pieces of clay.
The clay became a sign of our life together, where one
person's living touches another's.

The hub of hands formed again. This time people were invited to speak a prayer for the people in the group that
they might grow in creation and enrich God's world. As
their prayers finished, they let their hands rise and
slowly opened their arms to the future.

Scattering

"Praise Ye The Lord" was introduced as their hands and arms
were rising. When the community was standing with arms
raised, we joined in singing an arrangement of the familiar
hymn.

The potter, who had been throwing pots on the wheel, came
out into the congregation and gave witness to what he felt
in the midst of the creative process and the risk that anyone takes when they choose to act creatively.

"Christ Takes Form in a Band of Persons" from the hymnal
COME SHARE THE SPIRIT, was sung as a chant, which the students
took out with them, along with the clay symbols.

Follow-up

A few weeks after the service, I talked with the campus
minister. He told me how many of the students had their
clay pieces in their rooms, and that some of them had
made their symbols into pendants that were worn to class.
"Create In Me" was apparently the right expression at the
right time. It was a service strongly built upon the
music and the resources of the community. It was not a
liturgy into which we merely plugged the hymns. The
liturgy grew as we understood more clearly the nature and
style of the celebration.

The worshipping community at Purdue University sings new hymns lead
by Kent Schneider and a group of student musicians.

CREATE IN ME, O LORD

Words & Music by
Kent Schneider

CREATE IN ME -2

Further Reading

CELEBRATION, Clarence Joseph Rivers. New York: Herder and Herder, 1969.

THE CRISIS OF LITURGICAL REFORM, VOL. 42. Theology in the Age of Renewal, Fr. G. Steffani. New York: Paulist Press, 1969.

EDUCATION AND THE WORSHIP OF GOD, Philip H. Phenix. Philadelphia: Westminster Press, 1966.

THE FEAST OF FOOLS, Harvey Cox. Cambridge: Harvard University Press, 1969.

THE HUMILIATION OF THE CHURCH, Albert H. van den Heuvel. Philadelphia: Westminster Press, 1966.

LITURGY COMING TO LIFE, John A. T. Robinson. Philadelphia: Westminster Press, 1960.

THE LITURGICAL MOVEMENT AND THE LOCAL CHURCH, Alfred R. Shands. New York: Morehouse-Barlow Company, 1965.

LITURGIES OF THE WESTERN CHURCH, Bard Thompson. Cleveland: World Publishing Company, 1961.

OUR CHANGING LITURGY, C. J. McNaspy, S.J. New York: Doubleday and Company, Inc., 1967.

THE RITES OF PASSAGE, Arnold van Gennep. Chicago: University of Chicago Press, 1960.

THE SHAPE OF THE LITURGY, Gregory Dix. England: Westminster Press, 1947.

SOULFULL WORSHIP, Clarence Joseph Rivers. Stimuli, Inc. Box 20066, Cincinnati, Ohio 45220.

PART FOUR

CREATING LYRICS FROM LIVING EXPERIENCE

HYMNS OF THE CHURCH:
The Art of Writing Lyrics

> "Most people don't believe in the words of the hymns
> they sing — they don't even hear them. They like
> the tune, they sing, and they don't have the
> slightest idea what they are saying. Maybe that is
> just as well!"
>
> Bishop James A. Pike
> from An Address to the American
> Guild of Organists,
> June 21, 1967

One of the difficult problems facing the musician and minister is
selecting hymns which develop the drama of the liturgy. Too often,
our last-minute selections (trying to use hymns that "fit into
the service") reveal how inappropriate or out-of-touch with our
present world are many of the lyrics. The experiential world of
the hymnal and the existential experience of today's living do
not overlap anymore. For some people, that is the way religion
should be — separated from life, a refuge or sanctuary from the
cares of daily situations. For others, a religion which is remote
is not real. Songs that affirm a time which is no longer with us
are nothing more than a nostalgic trip backwards.

We need to search out those qualities of lyrics which will have
meaning for the people who sing the words. How empty is the
experience of asking a congregation to sing words that either
they don't believe or can't understand? No wonder so many congregations sing as if they are half asleep.

I would like to share a few ideas with you about qualities in
hymns that I feel are desirable for today's church:

The lyrics must be honest.

> Can we really say the words and truly mean them?
> Regardless of the style of language, whether a
> King James Version or a "street version," can the
> congregation sing the lyrics with authenticity?
> This doesn't necessarily mean that everyone has to
> agree with what is being said. Honesty includes
> disagreement. What is important is that the words
> would have some genuine meaning for the life of
> the community.

The hymns recite the history of a people.

> In searching for hymns that have meaning for
> Christians today, we should not think that we can
> only use the "latest songs." To cut ourselves

off from the wealth of the tradition would be a bad mistake. We'll need to build the foundation for our singing of who we are as God's People and where we've been as well as where we're going.

Within each religious tradition, the songs the people sing tell who they are. Songs are a formative power. They unify and clarify.

> The Black spirituals are an example of music that tells a people's history. The songs speak out a Spirit that won't die even in the face of death ("O Freedom") and refuses to be enslaved. They tell of times of trouble ("Nobody Knows The Trouble I've Seen") and a hope in a better land.

Spend a session with your community to select out those hymns which characterize the tradition of the people you worship with. Some churches use the time when people gather for worship to let members call out songs they'd like to sing. This could be a way of learning the history of your people.

The lyrics should be rooted in a shared experience.

Nothing is more boring than listening to something that I have no feeling for because I've never ex-perienced it. If what we are singing has no per-sonal meaning, then the manner in which the hymn is sung will be impersonal. This is a problem in many churches.

A seminary professor of mine once wrote: "The words (of hymns) should be impersonal   Public worship is a group expression. In private worship, the indi-vidual communes; in public worship, we voice common emotions." He is advocating that it is not correct to sing communal songs using the personal pronouns "I" or "me." It is not objective enough.

I have found that many congregations are tired of singing songs in the collective form. People are searching for the personal expression to be made in corporate worship. Meaningful worship always has a dimension of flowing between the community and the individual. We should not lose the sense of the person even when we sing our hymns. To choose songs simply on the basis of whether they use "we" or "I"

is a superficial distinction. To dwell totally outside ourselves leaves the inside hollow; to live
only inside myself makes me lose sight of the world
I seek to serve. Our hymns must be rooted in a
shared experience so that, individually, a person can
affirm the lyric's meaning and we, as a community,
can affirm the song together.

> I find it significant that so many of the
> Black Spirituals speak of a personal re-
> lationship with God. I was told by a Black
> Church musician that the people don't sing
> "we" since they're all singing "I" together.
> That in making a personal affirmation to-
> gether, the feeling of unity is much stronger
> than if they had made a collective statement
> and really didn't believe it personally.
> Perhaps the song "We Shall Overcome" might
> have been sung "I Will Overcome."

The words should be singable.

> Bad music will wipe out good words. This is so
> obvious I don't think it needs any elaboration.
> We'll get into building melodies in the next chap-
> ter.

We need lyrics that speak of today's world condition.

> It has always saddened me to see many churches that
> are culturally, politically and artistically very
> active during the week come together on Sunday and
> sing hymns that have nothing to do with the ministry
> that they have chosen to risk themselves in. It is
> senseless for a church involved in the urban city to
> sing only about the rural pastoral scene. Who is
> writing the hymns that affirm God's Presence in the
> midst of steel girders and high-rise buildings?
> Where are the hymns that give us insight into the
> Kingdom of God in our own time? Where are the hymns
> that teach us of Christ who walked among us and felt
> many of the same joys and sorrows that we feel? How
> about hymns that find the Kairos moment in the midst
> of the world rather than some far distant heaven?

> Our hymns can help us to deal with the world situa-
> tions in ways that sermons and readings cannot.

> And where are the hymn writers of today? They are
> in your congregation!

Further Reading

PROTESTANT WORSHIP MUSIC, Charles L. Etherington. New York:
    Holt, Rinehart and Winston, 1962.

LUTHER'S WORKS, LITURGY AND HYMNS, Ulrich S. Leupold.
    Philadelphia: Fortress Press, 1965.

THE ORGANIST AND HYMN PLAYING, Austin C. Lovelace. Nash-
    ville: Abingdon Press, 1962.

WORDS, MUSIC AND THE CHURCH, Erik Routley. Nashville:
    Abingdon Press, 1968.

LYRICS ARE ROOTED IN EXPERIENCE

I have always been interested in knowing how songs grow within a person. It is fascinating to learn the source of a person's imaginative idea and to see the kind of struggle and transformation that must go on within the creator in order to realize the fullness of the concept.

I've found that, for me, the most memorable songs are those that have grown out of an experience. Often I'll find a hymn companion book which gives some of the history of how the texts and tunes came to be written. Doing this kind of simple research helps me to better understand the history from which the hymn sprang.

Many of our greatest hymns were written for specific occasions when it was important that just the right words be sung. Hymns were sometimes necessitated because the minister could not find an appropriate text for the event and so he wrote one of his own.

> The author of the well-known hymn "They'll Know We Are Christians By Our Love" is Pete Scholtes. He wrote that song in the early 1960's in response to the needs of his young people in the parish he was serving on Chicago's Southside. The youth wanted a Mass style that they could participate in through playing and singing.

> Pete's previous musical experience included playing tenor banjo with a Dixieland band while in high school. He had never written music before. When he had finished a rough draft of the melody and words, he took them to a teaching nun in the music department to get an opinion. She told him that he had written the notes backwards, putting the stems on the wrong side of the notes. Well, Pete corrected the music and taught it to the young people as the Missa Bossa Nova or the Mass of 67th Street. A Catholic publishing house heard about it, published and recorded it. The song, which was written because young people needed music that they could identify with, has now been sung throughout the world.

Writing from experience is different than writing from a theme. In an experience, we sense the wholeness of the event rather than just a segment. This gives authenticity to what is written. Drawing from experience gives Presence to the lyric. I find myself listening more intently to a song that conveys an experience that I've shared in, rather than a song that talks about generalities.

An experience is something that I've lived through. The
lyrics for telling an experience grow from within.

A theme is something that is given to me. I have to use
my imagination to try to get inside the concept of the
theme. If I've never really experienced anything re-
lated to the theme, it will be very difficult to write
something meaningful.

I've enjoyed the work of the late Jim Croce who authored such
good tunes as "Bad, Bad Leroy Brown" and "Time In A Bottle"
before a plane crash cut his career short in 1973. In an interview which was published in the Chicago Daily News (Saturday,
September 23), he told of how he wrote material from life experiences. He had returned to the music scene in 1972 after
having played New York coffeehouses during the late 1960's
and becoming very discouraged from the experience. In the
meantime, he did construction work which he felt helped develop him as a person and as a song writer. He said:
"Rather than picking a theme and writing about it, which I'd
more or less done before, I became a song writer writing from
direct experience — character sketches, things like that."

When I wrote the hymn "The Church Within Us," it grew first
from an experience that I had had. I needed to get my feelings
out so that I could deal with them. Music has always been a
vehicle for letting things out of me.

> I had just come back from a church meeting where I was a
> member. I was in seminary at the time. It must have
> been the Spring of 1967. I was a collage of feelings:
> disappointment, anger, frustration and hope. This church
> had just rejected a request from the local grammar school
> to rent the Sunday School rooms during the week. The
> school was very overcrowded and needed the space which
> wasn't in use at the church. The governing members of
> the church refused the request because "we don't want
> those children marking up the building." The children
> were Black. The church members were White. The sadness
> of the situation was increased when I learned that twenty
> years earlier that grammar school had welcomed the newly-
> formed church to the community by letting the members use
> the school's auditorium for Sunday worship.
>
> I returned to the seminary wondering: 'What is the church
> for?' My mother had always taught us that 'you are the
> temple of God and that God's house is within you.' The
> church isn't a building, not steel nor stone. The church
> is people who are alive.

The words and melody came together within the time of
half an hour. It was one of those writing experiences
where the music and words really flowed out freely.

* THE CHURCH WITHIN US

Kent Schneider

* Instrumental and Choral arrangements of this song are available from the Center.

SONG PAINTING

One of the basic elements in designing celebration is the creating of original lyrics and songs which speak memorably of our life together. As the staff of the Center travels around the country, we are more and more aware that people are dissatisfied with much of the published "new music for worship." The music doesn't speak to their situations. Ministers and musicians are bothered when they buy a new hymnal and find that only three or four songs are useable with their people.

I believe there are some basic reasons for this growing dissatisfaction:

1) Many church music publishers are simply not aware of the advanced musical tastes of congregations. They underestimate the ability of people to sing. One publisher told me that his company puts out material that is already five years behind the present, "because that's where congregations are musically."

2) People of all ages have a greater knowledge of musical styles (raga, rock, jazz, country) than they did five years ago. This increased listening has prepared the way for using various styles of music in the church.

3) With the accelerated input of daily information, people are forced to live with phrases and events on a short-time basis. What has meaning today might be forgotten a year from now. What does this say about our hymnody? Does it mean that along with our bound hymnals of the past centuries, we would also have a changing collection of hymns which address themselves to the present moment?

What seems to be happening around the country is that people are awakening to their own creative potential as contemporary hymn writers. This is a hopeful sign for the local church. I expect that during the next ten years we will see a revitalization in the music of the church through people who choose to make a stand as creative shapers of future rather than continue as consumer victims of a publishing world that says, "At best, you are five years behind the times."

WHAT COMMUNICATES: Speaking Words

Lyrics communicate through memorable images that awaken feelings and paint pictures in the mind. Such words speak about the multi-dimensional world of God and man in fresh phrases. Celebration's lyrics come to us, not in sentimental slush or as lectured sermons, but as authentic statements of people who have lived in an event fully. Powerful lyrics grow from human experience. They have a first-hand quality to them. Being-there is communicated.

The type of communication needed for celebration uses SPEAKING WORDS — words which have an originating quality to them. They say "who I am" in ways that no one else can.

Speaking words have a quality of authentic immediacy which is available and present to us. The writer is not simply parroting a clever phrase borrowed from someone else or regurgitating an old insight. The person who communicates effectively usually has something to say and can put it across in honest and sincere words, not trying to be cute, but simply expressing what is going on inside an experience as it really happens.

This style of first-hand authenticity is a recent development in lyrics. During the early 1950's, lyrics mostly communicated to the adult, post-war generation and not to the young. Recording stars were generally much older than the teenager (Mario Lanza, Frankie Laine, Perry Como, Johnny Ray, Patti Page), and many of the songs were but adult sagas trying to be young: "Goodnight Irene," "Mule Train," "Tennessee Waltz," "Be My Love," "Cry," "Young at Heart," "Hey There," "Song From Moulin Rouge." Few of the lyrics were rooted in the experiences of the teen world. The youth were a people without a sound of their own.

A significant shift occurred in 1956: Elvis Presley came on the scene. His style, birthing the rock and roll movement, was one that youth could definitely identify with. He sang of the heart-aches of young love ("I'm All Shook Up"), of fashion ("Blue Suede Shoes"), and hard times ("Jailhouse Rock"). Though most parents appreciated Presley about as much as a case of acne, their dis-approval only enhanced his influence in the world of the young.

Elvis' popularity spawned others (Everly Brothers, Jerry Lee Lewis) and encouraged teen movie stars to become singers: Pat Boone ("Love Letters in the Sand"), Debbie Reynolds ("Tammy"), Frankie Avalon ("Venus"), and Connie Francis ("Lipstick on Your Collar"). The whole concept of writing lyrics had shifted from the "moon-June-spoon" pattern to writing for a specifically young audience and their specific experiences. Still, however, the song writers themselves were adults in New York offices try-ing to get inside a young person's life style, a process which was becoming harder to do.

With the advent of the Beatles, this changed drastically. Their songs seemed to grow from real experience that was familiar to young people around the world: searching, questioning, being alone, encountering different kinds of people. They used language which was common to daily life and not contrived. A host of other groups began writing their own material and recording it, and, most significantly, people began buying it. The world was excited about listening to and singing new songs. For a rock group trying to make it, to fail to write their own material or to imitate another group was sure extinction. Music had become the work of the people.

During the 1960's, the people began to realize that music could be a powerful shaper of social awareness. Lyrics that protested injustice and discrimination became as topical as the daily papers. They served to strengthen and unify people as expressions in the midst of battle.

The depth of music's importance is a matter of history in the civil rights movement. "We Shall Overcome" drew people together much like signs and slogans would have in an earlier era. There were songs of solidification written by such people like Phil Ochs, Pete Seeger and Tom Paxton, among others. The lyric writers created out of their own experiences, giving reactions to events and personalizing the struggle.

Generations of Black blues singers, people who had been overlooked by the White culture, spoke out of personal experience in trying to focus our attention on the sickness that was going on in our land. Working in the styles of the Afro-American gospels, spirituals and rhythm and blues, these singers would create lyrics to meet the needs of each occasion. In reality, they were trying to set life to music so we could sing about it instead of moan.

The protest music of the 60's was calling this nation to a radical honesty of where we were going. Like prophets, musicians took on the politicians of the time and challenged our consciousness about racial prejudice and war. "Do you think they're listening?" asked Bob Dylan at the March on Washington in 1963. He was pointing to the White House.

> "You are to them like one who sings love songs
> with a beautiful voice and plays well on an
> instrument, for they hear what you say, but
> they will not do it. When this comes — and
> come it will! — then they will know that a
> prophet has been among them."
>
> Ezekial 33:32-33

Music is the pulse of a nation. If you want to know what's happening, listen to what the musicians are saying.

Recommended Listening

BOB DYLAN
    Bringing It All Back Home: Columbia
    Blonde on Blonde: Columbia
    Dylan and The Band On Tour: Asylum/Elektra

JONI MITCHELL
    Blue: Reprise
    Court and Spark: Asylum/Elektra

DON McLEAN
    American Pie: United Artists
    Don McLean: United Artists

RANDY NEWMAN
    Live at the Bitter End: Reprise
    Sail Away: Reprise

STEVIE WONDER
    Innervisions: Motown

BRUCE SPRINGSTEEN
    The Wild, the Innocent and the E Street Shuffle: Columbia

LAURA NYRO
    The First Songs: Columbia

NINA SIMONE
    Silk and Soul: RCA Victor

Further Reading

A PRACTICAL DICTIONARY OF RHYMES, Lawrence Holofcener. New
    York: Gramercy Publishing Company, 1960.

IN THEIR OWN WORDS, Bruce Pollock. New York: Macmillan
    Publishing Company, Inc., 1975.

WEBSTER'S SYNONYMS, ANTONYMS, HOMONYMS. New York: Ottenheimer
    Publishers, Inc., 1962.

CREATING LYRICS

I encourage you to try a hymn-writing workshop with your people. You may want to do this in your home rather than at the church building.

Try to write something for a specific festive event such as Easter or Christmas. These are not themes. They are environments in which the events take place. You may have to help the people probe what new meanings do Easter or Christmas have for them. Don't settle for old cliché ideas. Push for what new meanings can be stated.

METHODS and MODELS

You will have to be sensitive to the group's needs. Some people work better alone; others may need to be stimulated by the group's ideas. If you work in groups, keep the size small enough so that everyone can have a chance to participate. Five or six people should be the limit.

A good model for beginning is that of <u>Journey</u> - a way of organizing images which follow in a time sequence that builds upon previous events.

Step One: Recovering the Meaning of an Experience

The object is to get at the main kernel of the experience by documenting the event just as it happened. Write out an account of the experience, talk it into a tape recorder, or tell it to a friend who will listen and catch some of the speaking words you use.

After this documentation, read or listen to the episodes. This time start asking yourself:

What stirred within me during this experience? What was I feeling?

Are there any clues here for understanding what it means to be a human being in this world?

What are the cosmic dimensions of this experience?

Where was the joy, the agony, the struggle, the creation within the event?

In this stage, we are trying to determine what this experience means to you and what it might mean to others. Is there a common quality of life that would enable others to know how you felt in this situation?

Step Two: Stating a Memorable Phrase

Much of our life is spent surrounded by phrases from advertisers, recording artists, political movements and television media. Each phrase is trying to make such a lasting impression on you, in such a short time, that you will remember what was said or you'll go out and buy the product.

Do you remember that cigarette commercial:

"You can take Salem out of the country, but... "?

The end was left off so that, in your mind, you'd fill in:

"you can't take the country out of Salem."

Or the songs that have the chorus repeated again and again:

"Stop and smell the roses" and "I believe in music and I believe in love" by Mac Davis, a song-painter of our time.

"All we are sayin' is give peace a chance" by John Lennon.

"What's the buzz — tell me what's happening?" from Godspell.

Composers of lyrics will speak of each song having a "hooker" — something that gets your attention and keeps you listening to the music for two or three minutes. Popular songs rely on developing a memorable phrase that can be sung over and over. The hope is that if you remember the chorus from the first hearing, you either will buy the record or listen to the verses the next time the disc is played.

Now, look at the meaning of the experience you've shared. Is there one phrase that stands out in your mind that speaks about the whole meaning of the event? Can you write the meaning of this experience and put it into a short phrase? Let this become your chorus.

Step Three: The Verses are the Movement of the Journey

Once the main feeling is written down, develop the stages of the experience. Can you select out one, two or three distinct movements that occurred in building this experience? What were the elements that made this experience significant to you? Let each of these movements become one of the verses.

Step Four: Reworking and Refining

What you have been doing up to this point has been defining the experience and giving it a recognizable form. Now you must begin refining what has been expressed. Here are some areas for work:

Rhyming is an art. However, most of us use the rhyme in a very self-conscious way so that our rhyming patterns call attention to themselves and become obvious rather than being subtle and mind-awakening. Many popular songs use rhymes sparingly, choosing, instead, to speak in a style of free-flowing speech.

You will need to do a lot of listening to comtemporary lyricists such as Hal David, Joni Mitchell, Lennon and McCartney and others.

Take one idea and work it through.

Most people try to say something about everything in a lyric when they write for the first time. You will probably have more ideas than you can use in one session. Save them! They'll become your resource library for future writings.

Take one idea and develop it with some depth. Get below the surface. Say it simply. "God loves a simple song" writes Leonard Bernstein in his MASS composition. Chances are that you can eliminate some of the extra words that just "fill" the lyric.

Develop vivid imagery.

Avoid the cliché phrases and words; those things we've heard over and over again. "Brotherhood," "love" and "hope" are all fine sentiments, but they have been

terribly overworked in our world. Unless you can give
them renewed meaning, it would probably be better to
develop fresh lyrics that allow our minds to interweave
with the meanings of the words.

We must get rid of the stereotyped and hackneyed associ-
ations of sounds and rhythm. Our words need to be as
spontaneous and as flexible as flame. We need to become
authentically ourselves and not artificial repetitions.

Know who you are writing for.

If you understand the needs of your people and their
experiences, then your words will have meaning. Once
you have lost touch with the community, your songs will
be "out of reach."

> "The cause of meaningless words in primitive
> songs lies in the antiquity of the music.
> The words become so archaic or their sense
> was originally so involved or symbolic that
> all meaning gradually disappears as the song
> is handed down from generation to generation."
>
>   Charles Meyers, ethnomusicologist

Every song gets the audience it deserves. Some people
write for themselves; others write for other people.
You will need to be aware of whether the lyric you
write can be shared in common with others or whether it
is better expressed as a solo work.

> A publisher friend of mine told me that he gets
> a lot of hymns from people who have felt that
> "God called them to write this song." Most of
> the work is either poorly written or too per-
> sonal to be shared by a larger group. He tries
> to encourage all authors when he returns their
> manuscripts. He tells them that some songs are
> to be shared with people and that some songs are
> to be shared only with God.

Listening will develop your ability.

Read through the lyrics of songs that mean something to
you. Analyze them. Check the rhyming pattern, if
there is one. What kind of imagery is used?

TWO WORKSHOP EXAMPLES

The following examples of lyrics grew out of two workshop experiences. I feel that they are good expressions of the <u>Journey</u> model.

VIVA LA HUELGA

<u>The Experience</u>

Sr. Mary Therese Gillespie: "I found the process of composing lyrics very difficult. Poor experiences with creative writing in the past caused me to feel inhibited and quite hesitant about this enterprise. Therefore, I sought to offset this hangup by searching for a life experience that had touched me deeply.

"I recalled my conference with Cesar Chavez, the strength and beauty of the man, his concern for the sufferings of his people, the work of the strike and the cause of justice and peace.

"Pictures came before my mind, remembered words — landmarks along the way. I wrote them as they came, forgetting style and sentence. I was interested in what they said, the meaning they held. (When I tried to say them better, I lost the feel and shape of the experience, so I let them be.) My song is one on the march, to be sung along the way."

<u>The Writing</u>

Migrant men in harvest fields
Caving backs, sunbaked hours
Fifty cents a basket, crewboss deals
Spirits pulsing, fists crying, we sing:
       VIVA LA HUELGA, VIVA VIVA
       VIVA LA HUELGA, VIVA CESAR

Strawbed cabins, rats and vermin
Sprayed fruit, sickened bodies
Families starving, children dying
Spirits pulsing, fists crying, we sing:
       VIVA LA HUELGA, VIVA VIVA
       VIVA LA HUELGA, VIVA CESAR

Cesar Chavez, friend and brother
Picker of grapes, migrant leader
"Our lives are all we have," said he,
"Stand up, show them what men you be."
Spirits pulsing, fists crying, we sing:
       VIVA LA HUELGA, VIVA VIVA
       VIVA LA HUELGA, VIVA CESAR

CHILDREN OF THE LORD

The Experience

Phillip R. Friedman: "Most of us by now are aware of
the retarded child. Yet few of us have considered what
the retarded child can offer in an understanding of
God's Kingdom. Four of the last five summers, I have
spent one week counseling in a camp for retarded teens
held at Council Grove, Kansas. These experiences have
confirmed in me the belief that living and working
with the retarded is an experience in the Kingdom
come."

The Writing

     Children of the Lord!
     Children of the Lord!
     Each year they come.
     And though some are slow and dumb
     They lead us by their smiles into the Kingdom come.

     Refrain: Allelu! Allelu!
                Rejoice in Him who leads us by His children
                To our home, to our home.

     Children of the Lord!
     Children of the Lord!
     This year they came.
     And though some limped and wept
     They led us by their tears into the Kingdom come.

     Refrain: Allelu! Allelu!
                Rejoice in Him who leads us by His children
                To our home, to our home.

     Children of the Lord!
     Children of the Lord!
     Next year they'll come.
     And though we forget and think we are alone
     By their touch we'll know we're home.

     Refrain: Allelu! Allelu!
                Rejoice in Him who leads us by His children
                To our home, to our home.

CHILDREN'S LYRICS

I have always felt that children could write their own songs, for they share in life in a much different way than adults do. With encouragement and time, children in your church could begin providing the whole community with songs that they have composed. The following song, "Christ Is Coming," illustrates the patient and imaginative style of an adult who worked with three fifth-grade girls to write the lyrics for this Advent song.

CHRIST IS COMING

Janet Butterfield --Dottie Metcalf -
Kathy Wintergerst--Barbara Anderson

Kent Schneider

How This Song Was Written

The Center was conducting a ten-week course on celebration with young people at the United Church of Christ in Villa Park, Illinois. We worked as part of the regular Sunday morning educational program with young people ranging in age from 9 to 17. Two of the sessions were given to creating lyrics for new hymns. The children were encouraged to do some work during the week between the two sessions.

On a Thursday afternoon, three fifth-grade girls came to Mrs. Metcalf's office in the church. One of the girls had already prepared the "Hymn." It went like this:

> "Mary and Joseph need some shelter,
> they need it right away,
> 'cause the baby Jesus is coming,
> and here he is!"

The song was complete! What more needed to be said? (Compare with verse 1.) The girl shared her lyric with all the enthusiasm characteristic of a fifth-grader. Mrs. Metcalf thanked the girl for her contribution and asked the others: "What other things do we know about the birth of Jesus?" The girls were quiet. So, Dottie took out the Bible and read a section from Luke which dealt with the angels proclaiming the birth. She asked the girls to use their imagination and become the angels. "What would the angels do or say?" she asked. The girls let their imaginations go and shared what they thought the angels might have done. Dottie did the same with the shepherds and wisemen. The girls used their imaginations and the rest of the song developed. (See verses 2 and 3.)

Now that they had explored the scriptural account, the next step was to probe <u>what meaning does the birth of Jesus have for people today</u>. The girls expressed their thoughts on this and their words became the last verse.

Following a model similar to that of the <u>Journey,</u> Dottie asked them what feeling would they like people to take with them when they've finished singing this song? The girls agreed that people should be aware that "Christ is coming, and let's be joyful." This feeling became the refrain.

For a melody, the girls wanted something that sounded like bells ringing. The refrain melody is built upon notes that skip around, much like the peeling of bells in a tower. I purposely avoided a step by step movement in the melody.

The sharing of this song was also important. The children invited some of the high school guitarists into the next session to play some of the songs that had been created. We sang five or six lyrics that the people had written during the week. "Christ Is Coming" generated real excitement. In a few weeks, the Advent season would begin. The children asked the pastor, Rev. Paul Stiffler, if their class could teach the song to the congregation during Advent. Paul welcomed the creativity and the opportunity to involve the children in another way in the Sunday worship. Teaching their song to the community was a most memorable event.

I hope that this one example would encourage you, as a creative person, to work with young people in your church to enable them to begin writing songs that they can share when they gather. You'll be surprised at the growth and spirit that this will generate. I also hope that you will be aware of creative things going on in the Sunday educational program that might be shared with the larger congregation.

Sr. Adelaide, as Wobbles the clown, creates new music with some youthful church members.

A WORKSHOP EXPERIENCE
on WRITING LYRICS

The following is a transcription from a workshop with ministers.
Our total time together was about two hours. The first hour was
given over to personal writing after a brief discussion on the
nature and quality of hymns in the church. The second hour was
a time of sharing what had been created.

An Elderly Pastor

The Experience

I was on a hospital call on Sunday afternoon to a lady
named Grandma Grace. She is 87 years old and is a heart
patient. I sensed her need for spiritual depth, so I
said: 'I would have been very happy if you could have
been at service this morning so you could have heard the
sermon. I preached on the Holy Spirit.' Her face lit
up and she said: 'You know, I taught Sunday School
for many years. Then one day I discovered that I really
wasn't a Christian. I didn't know Christ personally.
Then one day the glory came.'

Then I said: 'Grandma Grace, when you give a testimony,
you're simply beautiful!' That's why I titled this
writing, "Salvation Is Beautiful."

The Writing

> She taught the children so many years
>   of Adam and Eve and Noah and the flood,
> She taught of Jesus, the Son of God,
>   who healed the sick and for sinners
>   shed his blood.
>
> Her busy world of family, love and care,
>   so little time for introspection, rare.
> In a moment of sudden clarity:
>   the Christ she taught was a stranger yet.
> How could it be? Oh, how could it be?
>
> Her heart was filled with sad and woe.
>   "The Christ I claimed, I do not know."
> Turmoil, distress, heart-rendering grief.
>   "Oh Lord, Oh Christ, I seek relief."
>
> Her desire for peace, embraced in prayer,
>   Sensed response from Heaven, the God-head there.
> The glory came and the victory was won,
>   Glory be to the Father, the Holy Spirit and the Son.

A MILITARY CHAPLAIN

The Experience

I wrote this out of the experience of military people who
have to leave their families for days or weeks. I've
tried to give some of the underlying faith in God that holds
families together during these periods of separation. I've
developed this by first sharing my feelings of joy and
happiness in being together, then the lonliness and temp-
tation which comes with separation. Our family trusts in
each other and the hope exists that joy will return when
we are united again.

The Writing

    Is it Daddy's day off? Is it Daddy's day off?
    Yes, honey, it's Daddy's day off.
    Daddy, can you play with me? Daddy, can you play with me?
    Yes, I can play with you. What would you like me to do?

    Will Daddy be back, Mommy? Will Daddy be back?
    Yes, my son, Daddy will be back.
    When will Daddy be back, Mom? When will Daddy be back?
    Daddy will be back soon, my boy. Daddy will be back soon.

    How quiet the house, how empty the bed.
    Dear Lord, without my man I might as well be dead.
    Help me for the sake of the boy, to keep my cool and
        not play the part of the fool.

    Memories of the past keep surfacing in my mind.
    Pleasant thoughts of the good times and of hard times,
        but all times we were sure of each other.

(The chaplain was in tears by the end of his reading. He shared
that this kind of experience happened in his own family and in
the lives of men who had gone overseas. He felt that the church
had forgotten the needs of the Christian in military service.)

A MINISTER BECOMES A GRANDFATHER

The Experience

This is just my feelings about becoming a new grandfather.
I want to share the levity and the joy that moves from the
ridiculous to the sublime that my wife and I felt as we saw
our children growing up and beginning a family of their own.
The real joy, for me, came when I saw the smile on my precious grandchild.

The Writing

Joy, joy, joy.
Will it be a girl or a boy?
Joy, joy.
Daddy will buy a new toy.

They stood up before the preacher,
He said the words, as we all prayed.
Come kiss the bride.
Come kiss the groom.

No time was right, and would this be wrong?
Some say they had waited far too long.
Come, let's make sure.
Come, Doc, I was right!

They announced it for all the world to hear.
She knitted booties, and he told the boys.
Come to our dream,
Come to our world.

The call was anxious, and we all ran.
He drove the car, and she counted hard.
Come run with us,
Come park the car.

Tina, Tina, Tina. She's all red and all puckered up.
Tina, Tina, Tina. Wrapped up, her eyes shut tight.
Come, hold her, Mom!
Come, hold her, Dad!

I stopped by and knocked on the door.
I looked up with a start. A stranger standing there.
Come, she's here,
Come, Tina's over there.

There she lay on Mother's lap, Madonna so full of
        joyous love.
Come, see the Queen. Come, say a prayer.

Daddy's all proud, and Momma, too.
Tell the whole world, a sign will never do.

Come, help celebrate. Come, help consecrate.
She'll be baptized one of these days.
We'll tell the world, our Tina's great.
Come, sing a prayer. Come, help dedicate.

A MINISTER WHO HAS KNOWN DEATH

The Experience

This past summer, my father and my wife were killed. Out of this tragic experience I have had to re-evaluate life. I've had to grow a lot. I know that life is real and that there is pain.

The Writing

I am a song that is singing.
I am laughter that is laughing.
I am life that is living.
I am hope that is hoping.
I am flaming fire that never fades.
I am and want to be.

I am creative and always will be.

I live, that is honest.
I live, that is true.
I live, that is good.
I live, that is happiness.
I am flaming fire that never fades.
I am and want to be.

I am creative and always will be.

I am free and that is life.
I am now and that is today.
I am happy and that is joy.
I am real and that is pain.
I am flaming fire that never dies.
I am and want to be.

I am creating and always will be.

From these workshop experiences come beginnings. People start to
sense that they can deal with the meanings of their experiences in
a way that will have communicative power for other people. I would
not say that these writings are necessarily hymns that are meant to
be sung. Some of them are prayers, statements of a life encountered.
They are probably too personal, at this stage, to be appropriately
sung within a community. They are beginnings, evidence that something inside has been set free so that others might share the joy
and the hurt.

Like any language, if we are going to be able to speak it, we must
discipline ourselves to learn how to communicate through it.
Writing is the same way. We must practice letting our ideas flow
through us onto paper or onto a tape recorder. We need to do
this often or else the expressive dimension of ourselves will
grow dull through disuse.

It has been my experience that once people sense their own
possibilities and have received encouragement from others to
keep writing, they begin creating some very poetic statements
of life. We need to grow our congregations in this way. We
need to hear the Gospel of God's Presence as it is being written
today.

"I Write Two Hymns a Month"...

What do you do when you need a particular hymn
and it's not in the hymn book?

You write your own!

More and more, ministers and church musicians are realizing that
they are capable of producing some of the hymns that their people
can sing. If a worship service calls for a certain style of hymn
expression, they write the words and create the music. Historic-
ally, this is how many of our hymns have come into being.

Reverend Phil Johnson, a young minister with the United Church
of Canada, is one of many people I know who is writing hymns
for his congregation. The following is an interview with Phil
at Five Oaks in Paris, Ontario (January, 1976).

Kent: Phil, how did you start writing hymns for your
church?

Phil: It started about a year and a half ago. I had an
experience of confidence because someone heard a
piece that I had written and said, "that was alright. Why don't you do some more?" That's
where the creative process began for me. Its
roots were in the community of faith — people
around me saying: "Yes, we like what you're doing.
Let's hear some more."

I was sort of conned into beginning to write. A
friend of mine, James Brown, who is an organist
in Bradford, came to me one Sunday after the service and started asking me some very nebulous
questions, like: "What do young people like to
listen to, musically?" He asked all sorts of
questions that he should have had the answers to.

About three weeks later, Jim phoned me from his
studio and said that a group of people wanted to
come to my house and meet me. I asked him, "Well,
what about?" He said that he would tell me when
they got there. This was at 11:00 p.m. and I was
in my pajamas, ready for bed. Well, they came
over anyway. It was the 50th Anniversary of the
United Church Music Commission and they had rented
this church hall, chosen dates for performances
and were looking for someone to write music. I
said: "Well, you need someone to write the lyrics."
I'd fallen into the trap. They said: "That's why
we're here. We need the lyrics in six weeks."

I had never written anything like a musical before.
As I saw this whole thing looming on the horizon,
I thought that they had misplaced their confidence.
At 2:00 in the morning, I felt that I should give
in to the spirit, and I said, "OK, I'll try it."
They baited me along, saying that they would get
a replacement for me in the pulpit for three weeks
(which they never did), and that I'd have two
weeks off and that they'd find somebody to do my
pastoral calls (which never happened). But, anyway, I fell for it and started to write.

I felt really frustrated because I had never done
anything of this scope before and with as many
people as we hoped would be involved (over 100).

My difficulty was that I really couldn't accept my
own ability and say, "alright, that was OK, that
was good." I had been taught that you present
what you do and then wait for other people to clap
and say, "that was good."

I was feeling down about what I was doing. Yet,
I wrote the first two pieces which eventually
became the musical "Benji." I felt bad about
them because I knew that I wasn't going anywhere.
I listened to records and I read books about
writing. I talked with people to see if I could
get some ideas. I thought that I was at the end
of my tether.

I went to James' studio. In the meantime, he had
been over to my office and picked up the two pieces
off of my desk and had taken them back to his
studio. When I arrived, I said, "James, there is
no way we can do this. I am frustrated and I can't
go any further with it." Then, he said, "Do you
want to hear what your first two things sound like?"
I swallowed hard, sat down and had an intense emotional experience in finding that my rough drafts
had become music. I left his office on "Cloud Nine"
and finished the lyrics in the six weeks that I had
left. The last piece was written the day before
the performance.

This whole thing was a great spiritual experience. I guess that's how I grew to have some confidence in what I was doing.

Kent: How does the creative process work with you, Phil?

Phil: I am an individual. What I like to do is to work at things, but, also, to let the mechanism that's me just deal with things, too. I use my sleeping time for my creative thought. Before I go to bed, I put a thought in my head and I just sleep on it. Once every two weeks, I have to get up and write. There's no way I can rest. For the moment, I can see right down the path — right to the very end of it. That's a fortunate gift for me. The hard part is when I've got the idea. How do I put it into words? I know what the words are, but it's getting them down in the right places. For me, that's exciting — the bright ray of inspiration. Then comes the blood, sweat and tears. It looks rotten and it is rotten. I have to do some cleaning up.

Right now, we're working on music for Pentecost Sunday. I think what I will do is write everything I know about Pentecost. Every Tuesday, when I go to the office, I'll take out the folder and just keep on jotting down ideas, so that, in a few weeks' time, when I'm ready to get down to business, there will be a whole lot of things there that I can really work at.

There is a definite discipline to my writing. But, my mind and my heart do the dirty work behind the scenes and I sort of pick it up.

Kent: Where do you get your ideas?

Phil: I find ideas in things that happen to me. The last thing I wrote was a few weeks ago. I missed my train to Toronto — that happens on occasion. But, this time I was frustrated because the cab was ten minutes late and I was late for everything. I got to the train station and I still had time that I hadn't planned on. The experience of saying to myself, "I missed that damn train and I am going to be late for the meeting. Things will be half over when I get there" led me into writing about the sounds of just being at a train station. It's probably not the most reverent song. It's about the urinals and the sound of the constant flushing when you're sitting in the railroad station. There's a certain regularity and rhythm to that sort of thing. So, I wrote about the rhythm of life that I sensed there and of the sounds of creation. The guy who was pounding the tickets — that was a sound I'd never heard before.

I also get a lot out of watching the faces of children I love and how I relate to them and how they relate to me. I get a lot of inspiration from them.

Kent: After you write the lyrics, how are they transformed into melodies? Do you give them to somebody?

Phil: If it's a free-wheeling song, I don't worry about meter. I just lay it on any friend who will take the words and write the music. If it's a hymn, I came to the conclusion that you write a meter that is regular so that you can choose from a wide variety of tunes. The problem is that I wrote a piece with a meter of 12/12 or 11/13, which is not your regular meter. As a result, it has never been sung. So, I came to the conclusion that I would have to re-write it. When I did re-write it, it came out in 11/11 time, which is not your average meter either. So, I have come to the place where I write a first line and a second line, and if that fits a pattern I just follow it and the whole thing flows right along.

If you have somebody close who can write music, that's the greatest thing. They'll write the music out for you and work with your lyrics. Usually, a musician will have to ask you to alter the words a little, which makes you feel pretty good because you know that they have had to struggle with it in order to get a note or two to work.

Kent: How does your congregation receive your writing?

Phil: Well, they receive it pretty well. They understand that the reason I would write something for the service is because I couldn't find anything available that said what needed to be said. I think people really appreciate that. They have come to expect it as part of the furniture.

I started about three years ago with writing hymns for the church. I had a backlog of about three hymns that were pretty precious. My first attempts were not great. People would comment and say, "That was a hymn?" But now, people accept my hymns. One of the most satisfying things for me is that the people use the songs I write out beyond our Sunday service. Other people pick them up and they send me their calendars with my songs printed as meditations. That's where the real satisfaction of writing comes.

I feel a little embarrassed at this point because I am really so like a newborn writer...but, I'm happy to share my experience.

Kent: I think that's what most of us are too, Phil. The reason I asked you to share with us is that I think it is helpful to hear from somebody who has gone a little bit further down the creating road than the rest of us. That's what the creative process is about — risking yourself in areas that you haven't really tried yourself out in, so that, perhaps, you can understand the struggles that others go through when they try to create.

Further Reading

THE CREATIVE YEARS, Reuel L. Howe. New York: Seabury Press, 1959.

EIGHTH DAY OF CREATION, Elizabeth O'Connor. Waco: World Books, 1971.

EXPERIENCING AND THE CREATION OF MEANING, Eugene Gendlin. New York: The Freed Press of Glencoe, 1962.

THE MEANING OF THE CREATIVE ACT, Nicolas Berdyaev. New York: Collier Books, 1962.

THE WISDOM OF INSECURITY, Alan W. Watts. New York: Random House, 1951.

PART FIVE

CREATING MELODIES

WRITING MELODIES

"Help in finding ways of making the singing of hymns more effective is urgently needed. The form has remained virtually unchanged since the 16th century; the music seems to reflect the styles of every period but the 20th century. The richness and variety of liturgical music stands out in marked contrast to the tried and true sameness of the hymn tune. We need some new ideas, some different elements to make the hymn more meaningful now."

Dr. David York, Westminister Choir College
from THE HYMN, April, 1971, page 42

Now that you've written some lyrics, let's try developing some music that is expressive of your words. Where do we begin?

As an example, try saying these words from Acts:

"We hear them telling in our tongues

the mighty works of God."

Say them again and listen for what words you accent. Underline these words. Now, if you were going to build a melody that would be expressive of these words, would the notes be long and sustained, short and quick, or would you vary the length of the notes for certain words? Write down what kind of mood you would want your melody to create.

Now, sing whatever you feel, using these words. You may want to sing into a tape recorder and play it back to yourself. What did you hear?

Sing the melody again, and this time try to visualize where the notes are going. Close your eyes and actually try to "see" the movement, the skips and steps that your notes take to form the melody.

Once more, sing the melody, and this time diagram what your notes look like. You can do this in the space below:

"We hear them telling in our tongues the mighty works of God."

Does your melody look interesting? If it looks interesting, it will probably sound interesting.

In a workshop, a woman wrote a melody to her lyrics. Visually, the melody looked like this:

She wasn't really happy with the melody. It sounded kind of "blah," but she didn't know what was wrong. We diagramed her notes out so that she could "see" what she was singing. I simply made the suggestion that she try to create a melody in the second line that would run in an opposite direction of the other two lines. The song would then look like this:

The melody that she then worked on sounded much more interesting, simply by making this one change.

Rhythmic Structure

A melody requires rhythmic variations in order to make it interesting. The hymns of the church must be rhythmic. I feel that it is a phoney criteria to claim that all syncopation must be kept out of the music of the church. If music is to recite the history of a people, then we certainly must be able to sing music that has some rhythmic life to it.

The rhythm of the melody will follow the rhythm of the words. Generally, you can begin by simply speaking the words. What rhythm do you hear?

Again, go back to our opening exercise:

"We hear them telling in our tongues the mighty works of God."

This time, note which words you would sustain longer and which ones would be short. Try some variations on the rhythm pattern to experience what that does to the words. Now, try singing your original melody, using some of the rhythmic variations. Which rhythm is most expressive of your words?

Melodic Structure

Most songs are written in lengths of 4, 8, 16 or 32 measures. The most common structures for today's songs are AABA or ABA. Here is what that means:

(A) The first 8 bars are usually the most important statement of the song. "If a song ain't got it in the first 8, it ain't ever gonna have it" is a saying from Tin Pan Alley days in which a song was sold or forgotten on the basis of its opening phrase. The first 8 bars state the melodic theme. This may be preceded with an introduction.

(A) The opening melody is again stated.

(B) This introduces a new melodic idea. It's called the "bridge."

(A) The opening line is repeated. A "tag" or extra ending may be added for a finale.

Listen to songs that you enjoy. Analyze the form that they take. You will find all kinds of variations. For instance, the Beatles' recording of "Hey Jude" takes the form of AABABC.

Now, try analyzing some of the church hymns. Note the melodic structure of some of the hymn tunes. Try to diagram the movement of the notes. For example, this is what "Praise Ye The Lord" looks like:

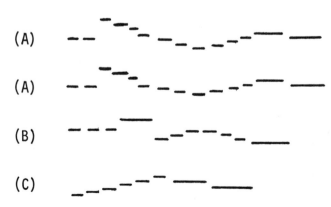

Creating Melodies

We live in a culture where we constantly hear music: when we work, go shopping, while driving the car. Because people have been exposed to music, they will have developed "an ear" for what sounds "good" and what sounds "bad." They can recognize when something is "out of tune" or "discordant" and when something sounds "pleasing." With greater listening experience, you can develop as a melodic designer.

Elements of Melody

The following are ideas which you can use as guides to check how effective your melody is. It will be helpful if you begin to think of melodic phrases as being like "waves" of notes that rise and fall as you design them.

Strong Movement - build upon the triad

Anytime you use the triad of a scale (do, me, sol), you will create a very strong momentum in the melody. For example, the first six notes of the "Star Spangled Banner" are built from the triad of the scale. The same strength will be present in minor triads as well. Refer to "The Church Within Us" in the chapter on writing lyrics. The first three notes form the minor triad.

Skips

A melodic skip will create a tension that can be resolved only by filling in the notes between the skip. The ear wants to hear the scale tones that lie between the two notes. Recall such tunes as "Moon River" or "The Christmas Song." Both songs begin with large skips which are resolved by the notes filling in the skip. A good composer will not immediately resolve the tension that a skip creates. He will allow the skip to linger so as to keep the ear hanging on with anticipation.

Here are a couple of pointers about skips:

A large skip will turn back by small intervals.

A scale movement will turn back by a large interval.

Climax Note

Most songs have only one climax note, which is the highest or lowest note in the piece. It is the note to which the phrase builds. Usually this occurs near the end of the phrase. A climax note may also be used near the end of the chorus if it is greater than the climax notes that have gone before.

Saturation Notes

When a person first starts writing, the tendency is to use only a few notes. Certain notes are repeated so often that they begin to saturate the mind like a drone.

Notating Your Melody

When you start writing melodies, don't worry about individual notes. Try thinking in melodic curves. Often a composer will simply "draw" out his ideas, using lines that move up or down. The notes will come later, once he decides the direction of the tones.

It is helpful to use a tape recorder when you are creating the melody.

> In a workshop on music, a clergy woman, who had never written anything before in the musical style, worked on some lyrics and then began whistling a melody into her tape recorder. She took the tape to a friend who played piano and he wrote the notes out and did the harmonization. If she had been concerned about what notes she was singing and had tried to pick them out one by one on the piano, she never would have developed any momentum in her melody. She would have always been side-tracking herself, trying to note down the tones.

Realize that notation is another art apart from composing. It is comparable to putting the glaze on a piece of pottery. First you need to get the basic form outlined before you put on the finish.

Collaboration on making the melody is a good technique for developing minister-musician relations. Here's one minister's account of finding a friend who could add a melody to his words:

> "I am excited everytime someone puts my words into music. There is a real spark that comes when someone is on the same wave length that I'm on. To me, that's a great experience. My faith intensifies when I see things deep inside of me. Writing is a beautiful faith experience for me. And, you know, my closest friend is a faith-orientated person, too, and that means that the lyrics I write and the music that he writes are not separated by any gulf. There is a unity about them that is an exciting process."

Freeing Yourself To Write

As you begin to write music:

Relax and feel free to express whatever comes.

Try to be alone so that your thoughts are not disturbed.

Don't worry about notes or writing things down at first. Enjoy the sounds that you are making. Try to hear the full orchestration of your idea.

Try to design out your idea in rhythmic and melodic curves so that you keep an idea of the whole piece in front of you before you start working at refining your ideas. This will give you continuity in the work.

Become An Analytical Listener

Develop your ear by listening to the not-so-obvious parts in the music, such as, the second or third voice in a section. Get below the melody.

Develop your eye by visualizing the music in your mind as you hear it. "See" how the melody moves. Let your mind become the orchestral score.

COPYRIGHT LAWS

The copyright law of the United States grants to any musician, author, photographer, artist or publisher the right to protect his or her own material. The copyright owner has the exclusive rights to reproducing such works. Permission to reproduce a copyrighted piece of music must be obtained from the owner.

The intent of the law is to protect the author in order that he or she can profit from the work. To copy and reproduce another's work is plagarism and theft. It is estimated that nearly one million dollars is denied to church composers because congregations reproduce the hymns on Xerox machines. The churches are really denying financial support to those people who can best develop the singing of the faith community. Some publishers are now bringing law suits against individual churches which do not observe the copyright laws.

Why is it that churches pay hundreds of dollars for Sunday school texts and yet can't afford to purchase 100 sheets of a good hymn tune? Many publishers are now making available single copies of their hymns. These usually cost only three to five cents apiece. Some companies also sell reprint licenses to an individual church which gives that community the right to reprint any of the company's music for a period of a year.

If your church wants to use some of the hymns which are protected by copyright, contact the owner and ask for permission to reprint the music. Don't be afraid of the copyright law. Learn what the law means.

How To Copyright Your Music

It is very easy to copyright your material. Simply write to:

> Copyright Office
> The Library of Congress
> Washington, D.C. 20540.

Request a Class E form for registering a Musical Composition. This form applies for either a published or an unpublished work. It also applies to new versions of musical compositions which you have arranged or edited. The words of a song, unaccompanied by music, are not registrable in Class E. Fill out the form. Mail it back to the Copyright Office with a payment of $6.00 and two copies of the work. Be sure that when you prepare the work that you place the Copyright notice © on the page. The notice must include the sign, the name of the copyright owner and the year of publication. For example:

© John Doe 1976.

WORKING WITH MELODIES

Often a group of people will pick a melody that they enjoy and set
words to it. This is a productive way of creating lyrics quickly,
since the meter is already given in the melody. Sometimes, a set
of lyrics will be written to a familiar tune and then the words
will be given to a musician to art a new melody.

Here are some patterns you can use to enable your people:

Interchanging Melodies

In the back of most hymnals is a section called The Metrical Index.
This lists the hymn tunes in the metrical categories. For example,
the hymn tune "Aurelia" has a meter of 7.6.7.6. D. This means that
in the first phrase of the song there are seven syllables; in the
second, six syllables; in the third, seven, and in the fourth, six.
The "D" refers to "doubled," meaning that the whole sequence is
repeated again. "Aurelia" is commonly used for the hymn text "The
Church's One Foundation." The feeling in these words will be
changed if a new melody is substituted.

> In a workshop, I'll invite the people to sing the first
> two lines of "The Church's One Foundation." These words
> are:
>
> "The Church's one foundation (seven syllables)
> is Jesus Christ her Lord;   (six syllables)
> She is His true creation   (seven syllables)
> By water and the word."   (six syllables)

Now, we'll try other melodies with those words to hear how
a new melody can change the feeling of the words. We turn
back to the Metrical Index and select out another hymn
tune, say it is "Ewing." We then try the phrase from "The
Church's One Foundation" to the tune, listening for the
difference in feeling, if there is any. Then we select
other tunes, such as "Lancashire," "Passion Chorale,"
"Webb," and I usually select "St. Kevin" as an illustration
that the words do not work with this tune. So, musicians
and ministers beware! Sing the songs through yourself
before you have the congregation try to sing them. Don't
assume that every text will work with every tune simply
because it's listed in the same metrical group.

After the singing of the words to different melodies, we
talk about the experience and how we can introduce this
into the congregation's repetoire.

Since singing words to a melody that is not the one under
which the words fall is often frustrating for the community, simply print out the words (acknowledging the
authors of the text and tune) and have the people use
their ears to pick up the other familiar melody.

New Words to Old Tunes
====

The March 1, 1963 issue of TIME magazine carried a Religion feature on hymns. In the article, Dr. Deane Edwards, president of the Hymn Society of America talked about introducing new hymns. He said, "We have found, through experience, that if you try to launch a new text with a new tune, you come right up against a stone wall. However, if it is a new lyric and an old tune, people will sing it readily." The article reported that Fosdick's "God of Grace and God of Glory" was tried out with a number of tunes, but only caught on after being wedded to the Welsh Melody "Cwm Rhondda."

Here are some examples of new words which have been written to old melodies. They appear in the hymnal "Come Share the Spirit."

"Amazing Grace"   new words by Sr. Adelaide Ortegel

> Amazing Love
> Come fill our hearts,
> And teach what Love can do.
> We need to find
> The way to live
> With arms outstretched like you.
>
> Amazing Hope
> That gives us strength
> To start each day anew.
> To spread the word
> That frees and heals
> That all may have life in you.
>
> Amazing Grace
> How sweet the sound,
> That saves a *(fill in) like me.
> I once was lost
> But now am found
> Was blind but now I see.
>
>
> *Fill in the blank with an appropriate word...something
> real for you.

"Come, Thankful People, Come" from a Thanksgiving Workshop in
                          Lexington, Massachusetts

            Come all people
            Sing along,
            Join our celebration song.
            Family members
            We shall be,
            One with all humanity.
            Push us 'til
            We fully share,
            All the pain God's children bear,
            Conscious both of joy and strife
            Truly celebrating life.

            Let us not be
            Satisfied
            When our wants are well supplied.
            Guarding what we
            Think we need
            Is a poor disguise for greed.
            Opening up our
            Hands and heart
            Means we also have to start,
            Over coming foolish pride,
            Taking other's gifts in stride.

            Come all people,
            Let's join hands,
            Reaching out to many lands.
            Touching lives
            Both far and near,
            Ceasing war and conq'ring fear.
            Family members
            We shall be,
            One with all humanity.
            May this be the Advent of
            Celebrating life through Love.

Setting New Words to Popular Melodies

In an effort to enable congregational singing, composers borrowed familiar
tunes and set religious lyrics to these melodies. Luther's chorales were
taken from folk songs and popular tunes of the day. It was not uncommon
to take a culturally-popular tune and reharmonize it, make a fugue out of
it or add variations. The famous Passion chorale, "O Sacred Head Now
Wounded," was originally a love song entitled "My Peace of Mind is
Shattered by the Charms of a Tender Maiden." Most people are familiar
with the ballad "Greensleeves" which is best known in the church as "What
Child Is This." "Danny Boy" is another popular tune to which religious
lyrics have been set.

The intermingling of church and popular music has continued even into
today. For example, a publication called "Sound - A Sony Student Guide
To Music 74/75" notes that the Beatles based their "I Want To Hold Your
Hand" on a section of Gounod's St. Cecilia Mass, and Blood, Sweat and
Tears have recorded a short piece by Eric Satie (Gymnopedie Number 3)
on one of their early albums.

With this kind of fusion, it is not unusual that the church would utilize
some of the better popular tunes to set new words to in praise of the
Creator. Here is one example:

"People of the City" by the Parish of the Holy Covenant, Chicago, Illinois.
(Sung to the tune of "Girl From Ipanema")

1 People of the city
    Gather together
  To celebrate our lives
    In the new creation
  In the name of the Father,
    and the Son,
      and the Holy Spirit.

2 People of the Lord
    Gather together
  To affirm our oneness
    With all the world
  In the name of the Father,
    and the Son,
      and the Holy Spirit.

3 Out of the forces converging
  Sing of the new age emerging
  Sing of the new Spirit surging
  In the secular century
  Creating a new history.

4 People with a mission
    Gather together
  To encounter mankind
    For the sake of the world
  In the name of the Father,
    and the Son,
      and the Holy Spirit.

"I WROTE MY FIRST MELODY"

The following song was created by Gayda, a dancer and minister's wife in Canada. She had never written music or lyrics before and she had a childhood history of being thrown out of rhythm bands and choirs. The song is a good beginning. It is designed as a call and response, with a leader singing the line and then the community responding to what they have heard. No printed music is needed for this kind of singing. On the next pages, you will read how the words grew and how the melody developed and was finally shared.

How the Words Came to Be

The workshop experience of non-verbally expressing my theology enabled me to crystallize my thoughts more clearly. By the time I sat down to write a hymn, I was able to articulate a theology from my life experience in lyric form:

I believe God has revealed to me, at various turning points in my life, that His Glory is Here and Now and is only manifested when I live my life to proclaim His Spirit in me (despite my human frailties).

I believe to proclaim God's spirit, dwelling in all of us, is to live in accord with His Divine Intentions: "to be in Harmony with God - with myself - with others and with the Earth." (Quote from Bethel Bible Series)

I believe I have the capacity to be obedient to God, but will, many times over, knowingly rebel and fail - not only God, but myself, others and the Earth (when I pollute it).

Yet, God's Divine Mercy, Providential Love and Divine Intentions offer me the necessary strength to try again; to live for a more "deeper" and meaningful life.

I believe the Glory of God - like the Kingdom of Heaven, is at hand and becomes so when I "live" out in fullness a "God-filled" life. I believe I become more "fully alive!"

My "aliveness" is my statement of faith and I try to "celebrate" this wherever I go.

How the Melody and Rhythm Evolved

While writing down my thoughts in lyric form, I kept feeling the rhythm and sensing the over-riding melody. I tended to phrase the words accordingly. Later, we re-arranged some of the words and phrasing for a better flow and continuity.

I kept sensing the rhythm as "birth....growth," at the same time, keeping these thoughts in my mind: we continually need to be "born again" in order to "grow." (The rhythm of life and the Earth.)

I believe I was personally experiencing this process of "birth....growth" during our "live-in" week; my body seemed to be vibrating these organic impulses, and my reaction tended to be revealed in the rhythmic pattern we evolved through my dancing and your use of percussion instruments.

In dance terms, the rhythm was accented on the first beat with an "and" count (impetus) and follow-through (2-3-4 count).

♪ ♪ ♩ ♩ ♩

one & two, three, four

The rhythm appeared to be saying:

> "birth - impetus - the gathering of energy
>   ready to "burst"

> "growth" - follow-through - release of energy
>   in space

(My movements for the rhythm were: gathering energy - hold - release suddenly which took the body through space in various directions and levels.)

About the Melody

Gayda had never written melodies before. Her artistry was in movement. So, I asked her to take the first line of the song "God's Glory is Here and Now" and to dance it out. Her movements took the following form:

(two twirling movements growing into a leaping exuberance).

I drew the lines of her movement on a blackboard as she danced out each line. By dancing out her ideas of what the words meant to her, Gayda was able to show me how she wanted the melody to move. I then translated her movements into a melodic and rhythmic form.

From this experience of collaboration, Gayda wrote:

> "I believe in the union of arts, and, in this particular union, between musician and dancer. 'Sound' is produced from movement and 'movement' from sound is equally produced for the dancer. Stimuli, in this form, offers to both the musician and dancer, a communion of spirits.

How Gayda's Song was Shared

As a part of the week-long workshop, we spent time sharing
what had been created. For Gayda's song, we built upon the
rhythm instruments we had (tambourine, maracas, claves and
hands), teaching the people the rhythm Gayda wanted (1 and 2,
3,4). Then a singer led the group, which was circled
around on the floor, in the song by singing one line and
inviting us to sing it back. Gayda was in the center of the
circle doing what she did best: dancing and being Gayda.

"I discovered as I was doing the song this morning,
that I can't do the whole thing by myself. I need
to say it and someone needs to respond to it. Repetition of each line is saying that we are in communication."

Gayda

THE CREATIVE ARRANGER

The musical arranger is a versatile person who can invision the orchestration that will make your melody line come alive. He hears the instruments and the setting that will bring the drama out of the words. With the arranger's ability, a good song can become a memorable one. With the arranger's talents, the musicians in your church, particularly those in high school and college, can become part of the musical ministry as they provide instrumental accompaniment to the worship service. Playing good arrangements is an exciting experience, especially when the charts give renewed life to some of the old standard hymns. You will enjoy listening to the Manhattan Brass Choir's album Praise to the Living God (ABC-607). The recording features numbers like "In the Sweet By and By" and "Beneath the Cross of Jesus." They are in arrangements reminiscent of the original intent of the music, but, at the same time, pleasing to the modern ear. You will also find my setting of "A Mighty Fortress" on the Celebration For Modern Man album (Center For Contemporary Celebration) an interesting arrangement, contrasting the straight church hymn with a jazz setting which is based on Luther's original notation.

One of the most creative arranger-composer-musicians, that I've come to know, is Floyd Werle. Floyd is the chief arranger with the United States Air Force bands and a church musician in the Washington, D.C. area. In the late 1960's, he began developing services around music in the pop idiom. These took place once a month. Attendance grew from 30 to 300!

On his album Now Faith (Murbo MCS-6017), Floyd comments about the new style of accompaniment which is needed if the church is to make the new music really effective:

> "The one critical aspect of good performance of these numbers is the accompaniment. For practically all church situations, this means a completely new set of priorities. More services, both contemporary and traditional, are ruined by improper attention to the instrumental back-up than any other single factor. When working with mainstream pop, the precision, and most important, the authenticity of the total sound becomes the paramount consideration if the material is to be of any value in a present-day ministry. The use of solo piano, solo organ, or solo guitar as accompaniment to choir or congregation, except for rehearsal, is not even to be contemplated. Particularly dangerous is to treat these songs in the manner of the now-too-familiar "folk mass" with the random strumming associated with these efforts.

"Essential to the effective performance of all these hymns is
one instrument — the electric bass or bass-guitar; secure
this player ahead of all else. To this, for the less rhyth-
mically involved numbers, piano or organ can be added if
the pianist or organist can count. For the rest, a third
musician is necessary -- a good, solid drummer. To these,
an electric guitar should be added to give the authentic
contemporary flavor to the overall performance. It is to
be admitted that this involves more than the normal sleepy-
eyed anthem involves, but pays off huge dividends; the use
of instruments is stimulating to the choir and advances
their proficiency to a remarkable degree, which will reflect itself in whatever they may sing, and the ensemble,
after decades of muddy and turgid organ, will be a welcome boost to the morale of the congregation. Moreover,
willing players for the requisite instruments are readily
to be found within the periphery of the congregation.

"We have already pushed 17th-century polyphony and 19th-
century egocentricity beyond any sensible limits, and
even the much-heralded "folk Mass" begins to bore. Only
the opening of the doors to a continuously evolving and
constantly replenishing form of church music, one which
composers can write freely and choirs and congregations
can sing with conviction and relevancy will guarantee
the survival of the corporate worship service into the
next century."

Further Reading

IMPROVISING JAZZ, Jerry Coker.   Englewood Cliffs: Prentice-
    Hall, Inc., 1964.

THE INSTRUMENTAL ENSEMBLE IN THE CHURCH, Helen R. Trobian.
    New York: Abingdon Press, 1963.

JAZZ COMPOSITION AND ORCHESTRATION, William Russo. Chicago:
    University of Chicago Press, 1968.

TONAL AND RHYTHMIC PRINCIPLES, Jazz Improvisation 1, John
    Mehegan. New York: Watson-Guptill Publications, 1959.

JAZZ RHYTHM AND THE IMPROVISED LINE, Jazz Improvisation 2,
    John Mehegan. New York: Watson-Guptill Publications, 1962.

THE PROFESSIONAL ARRANGER COMPOSER, Russell Garcia. New
    York: Criterion Music Corporation.

TECHNIQUES OF IMPROVISATION: VOLUMES 1 through 4, David Baker.
    Chicago: Music Workshop Publications, 1968.

CELEBRATION
MUSIC SERIES

This series is designed to provide choral directors, jazz instrumentalists, vocalists and liturgists with creative music for concerts, and religious services. The arrangements provide a flexibility for the use of various combinations of instruments and voices. Of importance in this series is the involvement of the congregation in most of the arrangements.

The following compositions are arranged for congregational singing with choral leadership and accompaniment by instrumental ensemble.

MIGHTY FORTRESS arr. by KENT SCHNEIDER   Price: $8.00

> This traditional hymn receives a new burst of energy when played by the jazz ensemble (trumpet, tenor and alto saxes, piano, bass and drums) and organ. The congregation joins the SATB choir in singing the opening verses with the organ. Then the jazz ensemble takes on a rhythmic version of the melody, featuring an alto solo. Part III unites the voices and organ with the jazz ensemble for a stirring final chorus. Recorded on CELEBRATION FOR MODERN MAN album. Arrangement includes 15 SATB choir parts, organ and jazz ensemble parts.

SONG OF THANKFULNESS by KENT SCHNEIDER   PRICE: $5.00

> A joyous new doxology to be sung by SATB choir, congregation. Accompaniment includes trumpet, tenor and alto saxes, piano, bass and drums, plus 15 choir parts. Recorded on CELEBRATION FOR MODERN MAN Album.

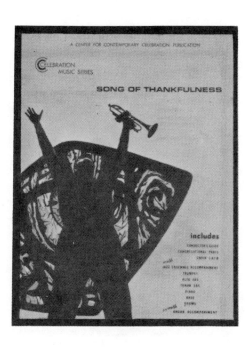

LORD'S PRAYER arr. by KENT SCHNEIDER
                    Price:$5.00

> The words of the Prayer are spoken by the liturgist with the community and choir singing the response "Be Present In Our Lives" after each spoken phrase. This responsorial style of the Lord's Prayer has heightened the meaning of the words for congregations throughout the United States. Arrangement includes: Speaker's guide, 15 SATB Choir parts, trumpet, tenor and alto saxes, piano, bass and drums.

Recorded on CELEBRATION FOR MODERN MAN Album.

CELEBRATION MUSIC SERIES

PRAISE YE THE LORD arr. by KENT SCHNEIDER   Price: $4.00

> This traditional hymn becomes a new singing experience as the
> choir and instruments lead into the verses with a dynamic
> introduction in a jazz waltz tempo. The whole work builds
> to a closing shout of "Praise". Arrangement includes: 15 SATB
> choir parts, trumpet, tenor sax or flute, piano, guitar, bass
> and drums.

CHURCH WITHIN US by KENT SCHNEIDER   Price: $5.00

> This internationally sung hymn is now available with the
> original instrumental jazz accompaniment that first brought
> the music to national attention. Arrangement includes 15 SATB
> choir parts, trumpet, tenor or alto saxes, piano, bass and
> and drums. A modulation into the final verse gives this
> favorite hymn a real drive.

AMAZING GRACE arr. by James McBride   Price: $6.00

> An exciting arrangement of this American folk favorite
> features new words written by Sr. Adelaide of the CENTER.
> An instrumental setting precedes the congregational singing.
> A flexible arrangement for trumpet, tenor and alto saxes,
> piano, bass, drums, and choir with congregation which can
> be used as an instrumental prelude in addition to the hymn
> accompaniment. Includes 15 choir parts.

BREAD OF PRESENCE by KENT SCHNEIDER   Price: $5.00

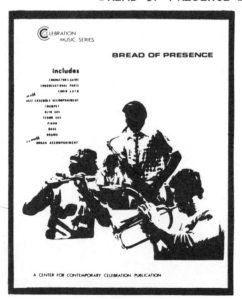

> A rocking gospel style song which affirms that
> wherever bread is shared there are no strangers.
> Can be used as concert piece with jazz vocal
> solo or as community hymn of communion with
> SATB choir, trumpet, tenor and alto saxes, trombone
> piano, bass and drums. Recorded on SONRISE
> recordings. Includes 15 SATB choir parts.

LET US BREAK BREAD TOGETHER arr. by KENT SCHNEIDER
Price: $4.00

> New words by Kent and Sr. Adelaide and modern
> chordings give renewed meaning to this spiritual.
> A flexible arrangement which can be used for
> instruments only, or with congregation and
> SATB choir. Includes 15 choir parts, trumpet,
> tenor and alto saxes, piano, bass, drums.

LORD, INSPIRE OUR WORSHIP by KENT SCHNEIDER   Price: $6.00

> An opening hymn which invites God's Presence to in-spirit our
> time of celebration together. With unison choir supporting the
> congregational singing, this arrangement develops into a dynamic
> singing experience. Includes 15 choir parts, trumpet, tenor and
> alto saxes, piano, bass, and drums.

Teaching and giving leadership to Church. Music Workshops throughout
the United States and Canada is one of the major ministries of The
Center For Contemporary Celebration. Through publications the Center
staff is able to provide the musical and artistic resources that so
many churches and campus ministries need to develop worship styles
that are meaningful and Spirit-filled.

PSALM 98 arr. by KENT SCHNEIDER   Price: $3.00

    The Psalm speaks of "singing a new song to the Lord." So let's
    do it! As the reader speaks of praising God with voices, a new song
    or with instruments, those sounds are brought in. The choir teaches
    a scat SATB line to the community and the instruments enter on cue.
    Includes 15 SATB choir, trumpet, tenor and alto saxes, trombone,
    piano, bass, drums.

CHORAL-SOLO ▐██

    This section includes choral arrangements with instrumental accompaniment
    and features vocal soloists.

ALL THAT HAS LIFE PRAISE GOD!   (PSALM 150) by KENT SCHNEIDER   Price: $8.00

    This piece is a sound offering of praise with all kinds of
    instruments and voices. Written for SATB choir, trumpet, tenor and
    alto saxes, piano, bass and drums, with organ and chimes. Features
    solos for trumpet and tenor sax. Recorded on CELEBRATION FOR MODERN
    MAN Album. Includes 15 choir parts and Conductor's Guide.

GOD'S FOR REAL MAN by ALICE SCHNEIDER AND KENT SCHNEIDER   Price: $8.00

    This anthem speaks of God in the midst of the city, in tall high rise
    apartments, on ghetto streets, in suburban society. Tenor or soprano
    soloist featured with scat SATB choir and accompaniment by trumpet,
    tenor and alto saxes, piano, bass and drums. Includes 15 SATB choir
    parts with Director's Guide. Recorded on CELEBRATION FOR MODERN MAN
    Album.

TRAVELIN' 40 DAYS by KENT SCHNEIDER   Price: $9.00

    A concert piece interpreting Jesus' time of temptation in the wilderness.
    Features rock-styled alto or baritone soloist, chorale duet for two
    sopranos, a Gregorian chant of Kyrie for either men's chorus or
    unison choir. Includes 15 SATB choir parts, lead solo sheet, Conductor's
    Guide, and jazz-rock ensemble: trumpet, tenor and alto saxes, trombone,
    piano, bass, guitar, drums. Recorded on SONRISE recordings.

THE CHILD by KENT SCHNEIDER   Price: $5.00

    A soulful song about children of all ages. Originally written for
    a baptism service. Arranged for tenor or soprano voice with trumpet,
    flute, tenor sax, trombone, piano, bass and drums. Recorded on SONRISE
    recordings.

THIS IS THE DAY by JAMES MCBRIDE   Price: $1.50

    A meditative prelude for soprano or tenor soloist accompanied by
    muted trumpet, flute and piano.

CREATE IN ME by KENT SCHNEIDER   Price: $5.00

    This setting of Psalm 51 is arranged for soprano voice, trumpet,
    tenor and/or alto saxes, piano, bass, drums and additional percussion.
    Soloist featured in glissandos and whole tone scatting with horn
    section. An exciting blend of the voice with the instruments. Includes
144 Conductor's Guide.

CELEBRATION MUSIC SERIES

This series features compositions arranged for various instrumental ensembles. Some of the works include parts for SATB scat choir or scat voice (where the voice is used as one of the instruments).

SOUNDINGS FOR NEW BEGINNINGS by KENT SCHNEIDER   Price: $8.00

Designed for use as a prelude, it features solos for any combination of horns (trumpet, tenor, alto saxes) with piano, bass, drums. Optional SATB scat choir adds fullness to the chordal texture. Recorded on CELEBRATION FOR MODERN MAN album (DS-418). Includes 15 choir parts and Conductor's Guide. Alto sax doubles on flute.

FUGUE IN G MAJOR by J.S. Bach arr. by KENT SCHNEIDER   Price: $8.00

This joyous fugue is augmented with jazz solo passages and builds to a driving climax. Arranged for trumpet, tenor sax, alto sax or scat voice, trombone (optional), piano, bass, and drums. Includes Conductor's Guide.

LOVERS ARE SPECIAL PEOPLE by KENT SCHNEIDER   Price: $2.00

A beautiful meditation in 3/4 for three flutes, harpischord (or piano) bass, drums. Composed for use in weddings and on those occasions when a "light" sound is just the right sound.

THE FAITHFUL GATHER by KENT SCHNEIDER   Price: $4.00

Written in the style of the Adderley quintet, this subtle rocker is a grooving kind of tune that gives maximum showcase for solo efforts. Includes trumpet, tenor sax, piano, bass, drums.

WOODLAWN WALK by KENT SCHNEIDER   Price: $3.00

If you have never marched to a 7/4 blues you don't know what you're missing. This chart is a joyous journey through street sounds and people passing by. Its title comes from Woodlawn Avenue, one of the most trafficked streets at the University of Chicago. The tune is a celebration of beautiful people. Features flute and flugel horn (or trumpet), tenor sax, and trombone, with piano-guitar, bass and drums. Solos are passed around. Closed with free-form improvisation for horns creating street sounds. Recorded on SONRISE (CC-400) record.

SOON A NEW DAWN by KENT SCHNEIDER   Price: $8.00

A difficult chart in a jazz-rock style of CHASE or BS&T for trumpets, alto and tenor saxes, trombone, bass, guitar (rock and jazz), drums, piano and organ. Solos for both saxes and trumpet. Trumpet duel closes the chart. Echo-plex unit for trumpet solo advisable but optional. The piece is based upon the writing: "In the last days the trumpet shall sound and the dead shall be raised". With this NEW DAWN there will be no sleepers in your community. Conductor's Guide included.

MOURNING'S GLORY by KENT SCHNEIDER   Price:$4.00

A trumpet solo with accompaniment from flute (doubles on tenor sax), violin (or flute), piano, bass and drums. Echo-plex suggested for flute passages, but optional. Originally, Mourning's Glory was used as the instrumental prelude for a Good Friday media event entitled, "Into Your Hands". A very meditative piece. Trumpet range A below the staff, to E above high C. Ad-lib and solo cadenza featured.

PHERES by JAMES MCBRIDE   Price $3.00

A 3/4 prelude for trumpet, tenor sax, piano, bass, drums,which sets a meditative sound environment.

GREET A NEW DAY by KENT SCHNEIDER   Price: $4.00

A 3/4 jazz waltz for trumpet, tenor sax, scat voice or flute, piano, bass and drums. Solos featured for all.

PROJECTION 29 by KENT SCHNEIDER   Price: $3.00

Arranged for trumpet, alto and tenor saxes, piano, bass, drums. Solos for everyone. Free form improvisation opens the chart and big ritard closes the piece.

YOU'RE IN THE RIGHT PLACE by KENT SCHNEIDER   Price $3.00
This is a jazz prelude for opening the minds of the community to hearing jazz in the church. For trumpet, tenor sax, piano, bass, drums, alto sax.

GOSPEL RAPPINGS by KENT SCHNEIDER   Price $3.00

A lively, foot-stomping "sermon" in sound for trumpet, tenor or alto sax, piano, bass, drums with plenty of room for improvisational "preaching."

CAN'T TAKE IT WITH YOU by KENT SCHNEIDER   Price: $3.00
A rocking offering of music arranged for trumpet, tenor and alto saxes, piano, bass, drums.

WE THREE KINGS arr. by KENT SCHNEIDER   Price: $4.00
An exciting arrangement of this seasonal carol for trumpet, soprano sax (or tenor),piano, bass and drums.

SILENT NIGHT arr. by KENT SCHNEIDER   Price: $3.00

A soulful arrangement of this Christmas favorite for vocal soloist with rhythm section (piano, bass and drums) and optional horns (trumpet and tenor sax). From a 3/4 meter capturing the stillness of that once silent night to an easy 4/4 feel, this arrangement will be a memorable sound for the Christmas season.

PART SIX

THE ℂELEBRATING COMMUNITY

WORSHIP and MUSIC: A Team Ministry

Celebration is like a symphonic tapestry with coloration and thematic threads running throughout the whole. It is the role of the musician and the minister to enable the various elements of the community to interweave so that the whole has meaning.

Worship is not a "hymn-sandwich." It is not verbalisms stuck in between songs. There is a flowing quality and a natural (spontaneous) growing to every celebration. Like ocean waves, one element of the liturgy focuses our attention as another element is beginning to grow and move.

> Imagine the sound of a segmented symphony. All the strings would play, then the brass, then the reeds and then the percussion. There would be no interaction in such a group. The listener would be missing the full tonal possibilities within the musicians.

> Imagine the weaver, who rather than weaving, simply strings threads from one side of the loom to the other. He doesn't take time to establish an interweaving pattern. Strung alone, the threads lack body and strength, there is no support; when the threads are released from the loom, they simply fall away.

These images apply to the teamwork that is necessary in developing religious celebration. Too often, the minister, the musicians, the readers and the choirs all act as loose threads that have not been interwoven into a meaningful fabric that has texture and colorations. Each individual, like a segmented symphony, plays his or her own tune without integrating the sound into a tonal community.

We need to build the kind of trust and team spirit within the formers of the liturgy so that same kind of trust and spirit will emerge through the liturgy itself.

A Clergy Conversation About Church Musicians

In a workshop in 1976, the conversation turned to minister-musician relationships. The clergy, a cross-section of ages and a mixture of female and male, were discussing how necessary it is to work with musicians in preparing an integrated worship service. Here is a portion of that discussion:

"I have a pretty healthy relationship with our
church organist, now that I am in a new church.
The last two places I was in, the situation was
kind of hopeless."

"Why was that?"

"Because the organist, I guess, was trained in certain
kinds of church music which were acceptable to him and
the college he belonged to. The music had to be in
the noble tradition of Bach, or pretty close to Bach.
The man I work with now, we have a good relationship.
Last July, we sat down for a day and a half and tried
to work away at what we wanted to do throughout the
year. We had originally decided to meet for only an
hour. How naive can one be! It ended after a day
and a half, and we've had several meetings, either
for a whole morning or afternoon, to plan what we want
to happen in worship. The result is that now I can
give him some words that I've written and he will set
them to a melody or find a hymn tune for them. He's
a rare bird, in spite of his fluctuating moods."

"Do you find that most church organists are tempermental,
sensitive people?"

"They may be tempermental, but I'm not sure that that
makes them sensitive."

"Well, what I mean is, do you find church musicians are
easily hurt?"

"I think anybody can be hurt. I wouldn't want to label
any one profession more vulnerable than any other. I
think that within the church there are professionals
and then there are up-tight amateurs. A lot of people
need to get beyond themselves.

"Recently, I've been interested in the stages we go
through to learn how to communicate musically and how
we can use music like a language, which is what I
think the church musician should be about. How did
we learn to speak? What did we do? Or, what did
people do to us? People said something to us with
the hope that we would imitate what was said. We
began by imitating. We hear something and say it
back. We try to sound like what we've heard. What
happens after the stage of imitation?

" We do our own thing. We put the phrases together."

"Okay, then what do you do next?"

"Communicate!"

"But what is communicating? Are you just trying something
out on somebody? Is that communicating?"

"It's receiving and giving."

"Okay, and that giving and receiving becomes essential. You
also develop your own inflections and your personal twangs.
You develop certain phrases that you can call on again and
again. It's the same way with the musician, but I have a
hunch that most of our musicians in the churches have stayed
at the level of reading and imitating what others have
printed. They haven't really developed to the stage when
they can express their own phrases and make their own statements.

"No wonder the church musicians will become defensive and up-
tight when you give them some words that you've written and
ask them to create a melody for them. You're asking someone
to draw upon their own ideas and feelings, something which
that person may never have done before. No wonder musicians
feel threatened. No one wants to feel inadequate for a job.
That's why the musicians go back to people who have created
music for the church and it has been accepted. Bach is
accepted, so if the musician plays Bach, then he or she will
also be accepted.

"But, look at Bach. He borrowed from folk songs of his day.
Some of the things he did weren't accepted well. We have a
ministry to understand where many of our church musicians
are. We have to recognize their limitations and their gifts
and seek ways of helping them to grow."

"So many of our musicians will look at the minister
with disdain if we ask them to play anything that
isn't in the Bach tradition."

"Why do you think this is?"

"Because it isn't churchy or religious music. It's
not traditional or not the best, in their thinking."

"I don't think we should speak in generalities about
organists because there are some around who are willing
to explore and experiment and then they run into a different barrier. They have three tenors storming out of

a rehearsal because you want the choir to sing something that's new. Too much of what passes for decision-making is based on what the majority wants and not on what is artistic, poetic, creative or exciting. There are some music directors around who are really exciting!"

"I often wonder what it does to a person to constantly sit behind an organ with all that massive structure. The organs are usually somewhere off in the back or on the side. We make the musician feel remote. And, that feeling of power is comparable to sitting at a switchboard. I often think that must have an effect on a person's personality. You know, if you put yourself in that situation where you have that much to control, think of what it must do to you."

"I never thought of that in quite that way. Another thing that just occurred to me, so often the organist sees the service through a rear-view mirror or a side view and so they disassociate themselves from the service action. They never feel the involvement that the minister does, either in leading the service or in being among the people. That must have some effect on the way they look at things."

"Some of the best services we have had with the congregation have happened when we moved all the pews and placed them in a diamond shape. The choir came down and we moved the organ console into the congregation. That way, you don't have any 'star performer.' The whole congregation is together. So often, the organist, and some preachers, too, want to be the 'star performer'."

"I don't think so. As a minister, I don't want to be a 'star.' That's a misconception that we have to do some real struggling with in order to find meaning in the worship experience."

A Musician's Conversation about Ministers

In a workshop, a group of musicians were discussing their feelings about their work in the church:

"The minister at our church wants to include me in the decision-making process, when it comes to planning worship and the music. At least, that's what he says. But, so often, it turns out that he is behind schedule in planning the sermon. He doesn't have his ideas organized soon enough so that he can talk to the rest of us on the staff, about the service. What usually happens is that he comes and tells me, the afternoon before the choir rehearsal, what hymns he wants sung. Then he asks me to pick out any anthem that will fit in."

"Well, the fellow that I work with isn't quite that disorganized, but, I too, feel somewhat powerless when it comes to having my opinion respected and suggestions valued. He says he wants me to help in making the decisions of what music we should use; but, my ideas are rarely ever used."

"I work with the minister fairly well. Every once in a while he wants to do something out of the ordinary, and I can go along with his ideas. He tries to make time each week for the two of us to sit down and talk over what's been going on in worship. We usually do this once a week at lunch. It's helped strengthen our working together in the services as well. I don't feel as 'out of it' as I use to. I know what he expects of me and I know the format of the service. I feel that I can prepare adequately for Sunday, once I know the direction we are going in."

"That sure sounds a lot better than where I'm at. This guy is a young minister, and he'll write some new hymns and then bring them to me at 10:30 on Sunday morning and ask me to select a tune so that we can sing it at 11:00. I just can't work that way. I keep telling him: 'You expect too much of us! What will happen if we try different things and we lose our entire choir?' I have enough problems with the choir as it is without the minister adding to the complications."

"Why do we have to be involved in the planning of the worship anyway? I'm a musician not a minister. I really play so that I can enjoy the worship without all this talk of involvement and faith and having to get up and bring the offering and holding hands. I just want to do my job the best way that I can and not have to put in all that extra time in planning the service. The service runs along okay, as far as I'm concerned."

"I'm a choir director. A lot of times there is not correlation between the minister's sermon and the music that is done that Sunday morning. The ideal relationship would be for the preacher to choose a sermon and for the choirs to find selections appropriate that will heighten what the preacher is talking about."

"A lot of preachers are just hell on wheels with musicians. They just always try to dictate to you exactly what they want you to do. They'll embarrass you in public and do all kinds of negative, nasty things. To give you an example of the kind of petty mess that you have to put up with: on Sunday, I was sitting at the organ when the minister stands up at the pulpit. He's looking down at the organ. We had just finished the congregational hymn right before the sermon to get everybody in the spirit, and we're ready to hear the message. He started preaching, and I was looking through the hymnal to find the hymn of invitation. In this particular church, the invitation hymn is to be sung by the whole congregation rather than just the choir. It's a time when we feel that everybody should be involved in the conversion process. If somebody is going to be accepted into Christ, then the whole body of the church should be involved and not just the choir sitting up there singing a song while everybody else is passive. So, I'm looking through the hymnal, trying to choose a good invitational hymn. All of a sudden, I hear this silence. I become aware of it and I look up and hear the minister saying: 'Brother Ray, would you please?' So, I get off the organ bench and sit in the front row of the deacons' bench. And, the more I sat there, I just got totally pissed off. I thought, 'Lord, there's no sense in my sitting in this church service because I'm feeling full of hell. I'm not going to get a blessing for sitting here because I'm mentally cussing that minister out. I'm saying inside, "What the hell is your problem, man?"'. So, after church, I asked the minister: 'Reverend, what was the problem this morning? I don't understand. Why did I have to get off the organ bench?' And, he said: 'Cause, you make me nervous!' It was at that point, that I decided it was time for me to go. So, I left that church and joined another."

Some Conversational Suggestions

From both of these conversations, we can see the prejudices and assumptions that too often the musician and the minister make of one another. The more wholesome relationships seemed to be among those that made time to talk and consult with one another.

Assuming what another person will say or what they will be receptive to is the greatest obstacle to effective working relations. Too many ministers assume that the organist will not like contemporary music. Too many musicians assume that the minister will not be open to their ideas in music. Ministers often feel ignorant of what is good music for worship. Musicians often feel ignorant of liturgics and theology. Making assumptions is an irresponsible excuse for feeling that there is communication going on. We can no longer afford this illusion. It is important that time be made for both musician and minister (and other people who have responsibilities for developing worship in your community) to work out the style of worship and music that will be most meaningful for the congregation.

I would strongly recommend a retreat weekend for those people who are on the worship and music boards of your church. Too many boards simply sit in judgment over what is being done without ever going a step further and offering some creative alternatives.

> In a workshop, a lady came up to me during a break and
> told me that she must have come to this workshop on music
> and worship under a misinterpretation. "Everything you've
> been saying so far has dealt with the musician. I'm not
> getting anything out of this. I'm on the worship board.
> So far, you haven't given me anything that I can write
> down and report back to my worship committee."

Do you see what kind of a gulf exists between the music and the liturgy? Do you realize how necessary it is to get your music and worship people functioning as a unit? It will be essential that your worship and music committees develop a spirit life together before the worship of the community will have a chance to grow in its spirit.

THE CREATIVE MINISTER AND WORSHIP

The minister, like the musician, is a communicator; one who is open to the workings of God. The minister, too, is an instrument, choosing and speaking words that express the intensity of the moment and the meaning of the history we are living through. As instruments of God, the clergy communicate the historical traditions, an awareness of our destiny as God's people and the significance of God's working purpose in our midst today. To dwell only in the past, the present or the future, when it comes to liturgy, is irresponsible. The minister must meet the needs of the people, which will usually cover a wide range of ages and stages of spiritual growth.

The minister is an originator, speaking out of personal experience. He or she communicates a Presence in worship that indicates "I have lived what I am telling you". There is too much second-hand reporting and quoting of books and what others have said that is passing as "communication" in the church.

The minister is an interpreter, a person who sees deeply into the times and the people that member the congregation. You get below the superficial and the surface of daily life and penetrate into biblical, cultural and social traditions that are being formed.

The minister is a per-sonal former, a performer, one who risks all that he or she is, in order that others might vision all that they could become. You speak a word of Shalom — a wish, a hope that each of you might be fulfilled and become more than you now are.

The minister is an enabler, a person with certain capabilities who recognizes that others in the congregation also have capabilities and qualities of inspiration and leadership. You are willing to sacrifice an idea for the sake of another's idea and personal expression because you can offer an opportunity for growth.

The minister is a shaper of ideas, a person who can put into dramatic truth what we've been saying in the congregation. You give significant form and style to the meanings of our thoughts and words. In order to do this, you are aware of the resources that the people bring as well as their limitations of time and talent. You invite people to share of those resources as much as they can.

The minister is a person of spiritual integrity and you take time to renew that spirit, both with your community as well as in private. With this integrity, you are free for the sake of others; you can respond to people's ideas without being threatened. You communicate an open-ness, a willing-ness to hear and try what others are talking about, but you're nobody's fool. You are together enough that people will know that they're not going to mess with you or trick you. You are together enough that you can give yourself away to others.

A minister is one with the gift of appropriation. You know when it is appropriate to speak and when it is not. Kierkegaard said that the problem with most ministers' sermons is that they try to say something about everything. The minister doesn't know how to appropriate what is essential for the people. So, to play it safe, the clergy will try to cover the whole history of salvation, quoting from scriptural texts *ad infinitum* while the congregation is mind-boggled by this *tour de force* of theological wanderings.

The Need for Flexible Leadership

Liturgical rigidity to either historical forms or to current fashion is not the way for the minister to see his or her role in worship. Within a given service, the role of the minister will be changing. At one point, the minister may be the one who invites the community to gather. At another point, the minister will be the prayerful leader, the spiritual guide. At another time, he or she will dramatize the scriptures, making us laugh as well as cry. Sometimes, the clergy will be the prophet speaking in our midst, raising our awareness of the needs of others and our responsibility to offer all that we have to meet the needs of others.

Clearly, the role of the minister in worship is more than one who speaks the words or "gives the sermon." We need leadership in worship that will be the embodiment of our expression and praise. Again, the minister, like the musician, has got to learn to go beyond himself or herself, in order to give per-sonal form to the liturgical action.

Does that sound like what the musician does when he is playing "spontaneously" or improvizing? Spontaneity is a characteristic of the church and the church needs your spontaneity.

> During the time of offering, in a service in Chicago, the congregation was invited to bring their gifts to the altar. The whole congregation moved up towards the front, bringing their money, banners, poetry, and one woman laid a trombone on the altar. After everyone was seated, the minister asked the woman to come up to the altar area. He could sense the congregation's curiousity. She explained that her husband had played the instrument as part of a brass group in that church. He had recently died, but that his death was no reason why the music or the trombone should not be played in the church. She was offering that horn to anyone who would practice it and play it as part of the brass group in the church.

Did the minister act "spontaneously" when something out of the ordinary happened? Well, if you asked him, he would say that he just acted "naturally." He did what he felt was right to do at the time.

In other words, he was ready to act appropriately when the action was necessary. To do this requires a discipline, for true "spontaneity" is an illusion. You must practice being spontaneous just like the musician must practice his instrument enough so that, when the time comes, he can play something on the piano that appears to sound "spontaneous." But what you are really hearing is years of work and learning to develop the skills to communicate on the spot. It is the same with the minister. You must develop the skills of effective communication and movement so that what is done will have the illusion of being natural rather than forced.

The extremes are obvious:

> I attended a downtown Chicago church. The minister rose and proceeded to read from the bulletin: "Good morning. This is the day that the Lord has made. Let us rejoice and be glad. We will sing hymn number 425." He kept his head buried in the bulletin like an ostrich who has his head stuck in the sand.

> The other end of the spectrum features the minister who is all conversation. "Good morning. It's nice to see so many of you here. How are the kids, Fred? Did the Johnsons have a good week? How's that new grandchild of yours, Mary? By the way, we're here to worship, if you haven't guessed that already." The style is self-consciously informal and there is nothing more uncomfortable than being with people who are trying so desperately to have fun and to be at ease.

As a liturgist, you will need to develop a flexible style of leadership that is neither dictatorial nor self-conscious. This will require practice at being yourself in unpredictable situations.

The Language of Invitation

The words that you use will communicate a great deal about the kind of person that you are. The first few moments or the last few moments of a conversation will often reveal the kind of relationship that goes on between people. The same is true of the liturgy. The words that we use when we gather and those that we say as we scatter into the world will reveal the depth of community that we share.

For example, what is communicated when someone shouts: "Rejoice!", "Celebrate Life!"? Those come off as commands. I'm being told how to feel. What is communicated when someone says: "Turn to your hymnals and we will sing hymn number 268"? Those words don't leave much option for interpretation. They are directions. The minister has simply become a signal-caller. A tape-recorder could have accomplished as much.

But, there is another style of speaking that I've found to be extremely helpful. It is the language of invitation.

The Scriptures give the insight into the kinds of words which Jesus used. He often laid out the possibilities of what we might become if we would take up the invitation to "come and follow." His words were not the exclamative and yet they were commanding. His words were not a narrow directive. They were powerful because they could be open to interpretation.

Jesus' words were event-filled. His words were alive with meaning. It was the theologian, Barth, who noted that when Jesus spoke his words were action. And, when he acted, his movements were illustrations of all that he had been saying. We need to regain that sense of event-filled-ness in our words.

Today's liturgy needs those kinds of speaking words that communicate, in a personal way, the corporate invitation to share in the celebration of God's Presence in the midst of the people. The style of invitation draws into the service those that wish to be a part of it. And, you have left the invitation open enough that people can share themselves at whatever depth level is most real for them.

The Sermon Event: Going Beyond Words

If it is of some comfort, you should know that preaching is not a dead issue today. Renewed interest in its many possible forms has produced numerous books since 1970 after we passed through the stages of trying dialogical, monological, logical, and even illogical styles of communicating God's Word to the people.

The sermon is not a gimmick to show how clever we can be. It is not a lecture to show how learned we can be. It is not delivered to glorify the one who is speaking or to serve blame on the heads of the listening congregation. Kierkegaard noted that the purpose of the preaching is to instill within the hearer the desire to go and tell the story. The sermon is the story-telling of God's work in the world.

One of the most effective communicators of God's Word is Rev. Paul Stiffler, a minister with the United Church of Christ, Villa Park, Illinois. Paul has a great gift for organizing a sermon in such a way that it becomes an experience, an event that the whole congregation can share in.

> It was in 1966, that Paul developed a "word jazz" sermon
> as a part of the first worship service in a jazz idiom
> that I played in the United Church of Christ denomination.
> He incorporated the sounds of the various instruments into
> the sermon to punctuate and illustrate the meaning of the

words. In 1968, he developed the story of "David and Goliath"
which we set to a walking bass line and blues interpretation by
the band. The sermon took the form of a rhymed pattern of
speaking. Here's how it began:

> "There once was a lad by the name of Dave,
> Who figured in a scene that was mighty grave.
> A little, old kid with a sling in his hand,
> Was to do a job that was made for man, Yeah, man."

> The congregation then responded: "Yeah, man."

The sermon, entitled "Slings and Solutions," recounted the
Biblical story and then moved into commenting on the giants of
our time that each one of us must encounter. The entire work
is available on the album, Celebration For Modern Man.

In 1976, Paul created a sermon event for the ten-year celebration
since the first service in jazz. For this experience, we talked
over the meaning of the whole service and the different kinds of
music and hymns that the band could share with the congregation.
We were also mindful of the fact that we didn't want this to be
a "show" or merely a commemoration of the past. It had to have
meaning for the congregation.

"In preparing a sermon," Paul said, "I try to be sensitive to the
needs of the people. I also try to be aware of the abilities of
the people in the congregation so that I can call upon certain
ones to share in the sermon-event. I often call on The Joy Singers,
a group of women in the church, to incorporate songs into the
spoken words. Sometimes, I'll integrate drama or the choir into
the sermon. It is important that I have knowledge of the resources of the musicians and dramatists so I know what they are
capable of doing."

In this way, the minister is able to maintain a level of quality
and artistic integrity which is essential for communicating and
meeting the needs of the people.

The following is the text of the sermon-at-large event which Paul
created for the tenth anniversary of our introducing new liturgy and
music to the church. Paul spoke the words while moving among the
congregation: down the center aisle, from the chancel, in the sanctuary
and before the altar. His mobility was a key to the drama of the event.
A very fine reader was invited to read the indicated parts. The musicians, choirs and vocal soloists entered at certain points, which are
indicated. The only people who had scripts were Paul, myself, the
reader, the soloist, the choir director and the organist.

HOW SHALL WE SING A NEW SONG ?

A SERMON IN SOUND   by Rev. Paul Stiffler

MUSICIANS	MINISTER	DRAMATIC READER
(Vocal solo on opening lines of "I Wish I Knew How It Would Feel to Be Free" by Billy Taylor.)		
"I wish I knew how it would feel to be free... *I wish...* *I wish...* *I wish..."*	DUE TO FEELINGS BEYOND MY CONTROL LIFE HAS BEEN INDEFINITELY POSTPONED... Like the man by the pool of Bethsaida, I lie by the waters of life, waiting for someone to put me in.	
	Sometimes the wait is serene. I watch the others in the pool. I feel confident that my turn will come. A loving God will plunge me into life. In the meantime, how interesting to observe the living.	
	Sometimes the wait is painful. I'm miserable here. I hurt. Help me! Help me! Somebody bring me to life! I've waited so long... Why doesn't something good happen?	
	The healing words are hard. "Pick up your bed and walk." (Page 62, ALIVE NOW, May/June 1975. Anne Trapp)	
		O HOW COULD WE SING THE LORD'S SONG IN A FOREIGN LAND?
	Sing a new song unto the Lord,	BY THE RIVERS OF BABYLON WE SAT DOWN AND WEPT WHEN WE RE-MEMBERED ZION.
		THERE ON THE WILLOW TREES WE HUNG UP OUR HARPS,
	For he has done marvelous deeds,	
	His right hand and holy arm have won him the victory.	FOR THERE, THOSE WHO CARRIED US OFF, DEMANDED MUSIC AND SINGING,
	The Lord has made his victory known, he has displayed his righteousness to all the nations.	

A SERMON IN SOUND

MUSICIANS	MINISTER	DRAMATIC READER
		AND OUR CAPTORS CALLED ON US TO BE MERRY:
	He has remembered his constancy, his love for the house of Israel. All the ends of the earth have seen the victory of our God.	
		SING US ONE OF THE SONGS OF ZION (THEY CRIED TO US)
	Acclaim the Lord, all people on earth.	
		HOW COULD WE SING THE LORD'S SONG IN AN ENEMY CAMP?
(Vocal solo with piano accompaniment.) HYMN: "It Came Upon a Midnight Clear" verse 3 "And ye beneath Life's crushing load..."		
	When all that we have lived for, stood for...	
"Whose forms are bending low...		
	worked for, prayed for...	
"Who toil along the climbing way...		
	saved for, hoped for...	
"with painful steps and slow..."		
	crushes us.	
		AND JOB SAID, THOUGH HE SLAY ME, YET WILL I TRUST HIM...
	There seems to be no end, no place, nowhere to turn.	
		HE ALSO SHALL BE MY SALVATION
	Yes, we are the aliens in a land foreign to us, where the promotion of good health, of fun and frolic, of success and wealth, everlasting youth and no death, are allowed... yes, we are the transgressors. We, who age, who are found by sickness and disease, who have nothing left after taxes, whose life has become serious. How can we sing the Lord's song in this foreign land, this familiar foreign land, this home place, this camp which has captured us, we who have dared to grow old, who have let tragedy overtake us?	

A SERMON IN SOUND

MUSICIANS	MINISTER	DRAMATIC READER

(Vocalist unaccompanied.)
"I wish I knew how it would
feel to be free,
I wish I knew I could break
these chains binding me,
I wish I could say all I'm
longing to say...."

O SING! SING UNTO
THE LORD...
SING A NEW SONG
   SING TO THE LORD
ALL THE NATIONS!

But how can I sing? My heart
no longer carries a tune.
I am besieged with life,
I cannot, I cannot...

*"I wish I knew...*GREAT IS THE LORD,
AND GREATLY TO BE
PRAISED: HE IS TO
BE FEARED ABOVE ALL
GODS...

I have everything I need or want,
I've worked hard, I gave my sweat and
blood to these things, my things, my
possessions, my goals.
I lived with them, for them.
They were the center of my life,
nothing squeezed in between, not my
family, not other people, not...
    not even God...and now,
it is so empty,
I'm so empty, filled, stuffed with
my things, but at the same time, empty!

HE IS TO BE FEARED
ABOVE ALL GODS!

Yes, it has been difficult to find
the way to go, with so many pushes and
pulls, so many attractive things coming
at me, I'm so alone in all of this.
The disappointment, the tragedy, the
frustration, the limiting gift, the
short time, they are my captors, they
have challenged the song that is me,
the little song I once sang...

TO GOD, MY DEFENDER,
I SAY, WHY HAVE YOU
FORGOTTEN ME? WHY
MUST I GO ON SUFFERING
FROM THE CRUELTY OF MY
ENEMIES? I AM CRUSHED
BY THEIR INSULTS, AS
THEY KEEP ON ASKING ME:
"WHERE IS YOUR GOD?"

A SERMON IN SOUND

MUSICIANS	MINISTER	DRAMATIC READER

DRAMATIC READER:

WHY AM I SO SAD? WHY
AM I SO TROUBLED?

(Vocalist, with band, sings:
"I Wish I Knew How It Would
* Feel to Be Free" in its*
* entirety.)*

WHY AM I SO SAD? WHY
AM I SO TROUBLED? I
WILL PUT MY HOPE IN
GOD, AND ONCE AGAIN I
WILL PRAISE HIM, MY
SAVIOR AND MY GOD.
                    (Psalm 42)

Yes! Yes! Life is mine!
There is a song in my heart!
It leaps to be free, it breaks the
chains that surround me,
     and what's the difference so long
               as I remember...

THE LORD WILL KEEP
YOUR GOING OUT AND
YOUR COMING IN...
               (Psalm 121)

I have a note to sing, and
you have a note to sing, and
we have a note to sing, and
     soon a symphony, a community,
that is not a single note, but
     a song!
               a song that is to be sung.

(Choir, with organ,
* finishes: "It Came Upon*
* a Midnight Clear," verse 3.)*

GLORY TO GOD IN HIGHEST
HEAVEN AND ON EARTH
PEACE...ON WHOM HIS
FAVOR RESTS.
               (Luke 2:14 NEB)

I heard that song, how covered over
it had become, but, it was there.
I didn't let it go. It was there!

SO THE WORD BECAME
FLESH: HE CAME TO
DWELL AMONG US, AND
WE SAW HIS GLORY,
SUCH GLORY AS BE-
FITS THE FATHER'S
ONLY SON, FULL OF
GRACE AND TRUTH.

A SERMON IN SOUND

MUSICIANS   MINISTER   DRAMATIC READER

He lived with us,
    He lived as one
of us,
        He lives with us.
God, you surprise me,
            always You
surprise me,
        how can it be?

(The following prayer was chanted
in plainsong by Paul as he stood
facing the altar.)

Be merciful to me, God, because of your constant love;
wipe away my sins, because of your great mercy!
Wash away my evil, and make me clean from my sin!
Create a pure heart in me, God, and put a new and
    loyal spirit in me.
Do not banish me from your presence; do not take
    your holy spirit away from me.
Give me again the joy that comes from your salvation,
    and make my spirit obedient.
Then I will teach sinners your commands, and they
    will turn back to you.
Spare my life, God my Savior and I will gladly
    proclaim your righteousness.
Help me to speak, Lord, and I will praise you.
You do not want sacrifices, or I would offer them;
You are not pleased with burnt offerings.
My sacrifice is a submissive spirit, God;
A submissive and obedient heart you will not reject.
                (Psalm 51:1-2, 10-19 TEV)

(Paul remained in prayer at the
altar throughout the reading and hymn.)

THE WORD WAS WITH GOD
AT THE BEGINNING AND
THROUGH HIM ALL THINGS
CAME TO BE; NO SINGLE
THING WAS CREATED WITH-
OUT HIM. ALL THAT CAME
TO BE WAS ALIVE WITH
HIS LIFE, AND THAT LIFE
WAS THE LIGHT OF MEN.
THE LIGHT SHINES ON IN
THE DARK, AND THE
DARKNESS HAS NEVER
MASTERED IT.
        (John 1:3-5 NEB)

Rev. Paul Stiffler chanting part of the sermon-in-sound.

A SERMON IN SOUND

MUSICIANS	MINISTER	DRAMATIC READER

(Vocalist, with piano, sings "Morning Has Broken".)

This is the dawn of my
new day,
   morning has broken.
                  I
celebrate this day with
my life, praise the Creator
who gave it,
   let all my days be
praise,
      let my thoughts,
      let my words,
      let my deeds
         be praise.
Let the song go out to all
the world,
        join me, join me.
Sing a new song!

                          COME INTO HIS PRESENCE
                          WITH SINGING!

Speak a new word!

                          DECLARE HIS GLORY
                          AMONG THE NATIONS,
                          HIS MARVELOUS WORKS
                          AMONG ALL THE PEOPLES!

Walk a new path!

                          FOLLOW ME!

(Solo flute begins playing underneath the Minister's words and keeps on playing as he moves into a time of prayer with the congregation.)

ABOUT THIS SCRIPT:

It is important to keep in mind, from this experience, that

MINISTER AS ARRANGER	— the minister really served as the musical and dramatic arranger for the sermon. He knew what the people were able to do and the effect that their artistry would have within the whole;

166

TEAM CREATING — in preparing for the sermon, Paul had discussed
OF MUSICIAN   some of his formative ideas with the musicians
AND MINISTER   and he invited the musicians to contribute their
                   ideas and resources that would nourish and grow
                   the whole work;

AN IMMEDIACY — the movement of the minister out among the people
AND PRESENCE   and into different parts of the sanctuary kept
                   the congregation within the immediacy of the
                   words, so that, when Paul went to the altar and
                   chanted the Psalmist's words, he was bearing the
                   congregation with him. We were not watching
                   someone "up there," we had some sense of the
                   person and we were <u>with</u> him in prayer;

MULTI-MEDIA — and this was a sermon in multi-media style. So
STYLE   often we think of multi-media as having to do
                   with slides and visual projection. Media refers
                   to everything that is around us. It is our
                   whole environment that we use to communicate
                   with. Some of the elements were familiar (such
                   as the Christmas carol and hymn), others were
                   not (such as the jazz instruments and solo
                   singing). This combination of the old and the
                   new into a totally new format was central to
                   the power of the communication. There was a
                   wave of anticipation among the people for what
                   would come next.

MINIMAL — and there was no printed bulletin. The only
PRINT FOR   materials that were given out were the song
THE   sheets for the new hymns. People had a chance
COMMUNITY   to see one another. Our focus was on what was
                   happening, not on what was written.

FURTHER READING

Experimental Preaching, John Killinger (ed.)
        Nashville: Abingdon Press, 1973.

Preaching and Community, Rudolf Bohren
        Richmond, Virginia: John Knox Press, 1963.

Preaching for Today, Clyde E. Fant
        New York: Harper and Row, 1975.

Speaking, (La Parole), Georges Gusdorf
        Northwestern University Press, 1965.

The Preaching Event, William L. Malcomson
        Philadelphia: The Westminster Press, 1968.

SINGING FOR GOD

> A singer cannot delight you with his (or her)
> singing, unless he (or she) delights to sing.
>
> Kahlil Gibran

To sing in the service of God is not a half-hearted vocation. It
requires that we give everything we have as "instruments of the
Lord." In the Old Testament and the New Testament there are
accounts of music being used in the worshipping community. Each
of the accounts speaks of a Spirit of singing that characterized
the joy within the people.

> "sing psalms and hymns and spiritual songs with
>   thankfulness in your hearts to God"
>
> Colossians 3:16

> "singing and making melody to the Lord with all
>   your heart"
>
> Ephesians 4:19

Such spirit must be present within the church musician who desires
to sing for God.

To sing is to give movement and endurance to our words. Singing
frees the words from a life of monotones and sets the lyrics soar-
ing and diving more deeply into the heart than words can go. To
know how to use the voice in an expressive way that takes on
meaning for others is a vocation well worth pursuing.

Every person has a key note to sound in life. Whatever this key
note would be for you, it would be a natural tone, not something
that is forced or mechanical.

> As a Brahmin studies the Vedas, he does more than just
> read the words. He will also take each word and syl-
> lable and pronounce each sound. This may be done for
> years. The Brahmin does not hear the sound once with
> his ears and think: "I have learned it!" He repeats
> the sound again and again until the sound and his own
> life-current are one. Again, the music and the singer
> are one in the same.

You may spend your lifetime finding that key note, that voice that is most natural to your own being. But, once you have found it, you will have found the key to life. Your singing will be able to help others.

> Ancient singers would sing one note for hours and check what effect that note had on their body and mental attitude. Today, people gather to chant the names of God (Abba, Yahweh, Elohim) as recorded in the Scriptures. They may also chant the sound "OM" from the Hindu prayer meaning "all life is God." People are searching for their key-sound in life.

As a singer, your voice is unique within the orchestra of God's universe. Your voice tells others about your own personal evolution. Just by hearing you, others will know your character, what motivates you, what disciplines you, what you live by and the changes you have gone through. Just as we experience vocal changes from infancy to old age, so we will also experience changes in the voice as we move into new stages of spiritual growth.

It is sometimes said of an electrifying singer, that the person sings with "soul." Ray Charles once defined "soul" as being characteristic of a person who had lived both the good and the bad of life and knew which was which. In Eastern religions, it is thought that the voice is the soul of the person which refuses to be encased in the material body and constantly emerges to fly freely in the air, to go beyond the body. This is what I was saying earlier — that in order to be an effective communicator, you must go beyond yourself in order to help the listener get outside.

> The secret in singing is found between the vibration in the singer's voice and the throb in the hearer's heart.
>
> Kahlil Gibran

THE PRESENCE THAT YOU ARE

Have you ever been in a conversation where you were sure that the person you were talking to didn't hear a word that you were saying? Have you ever been physically present in a room, yet worlds away? It is essential that a musician be a Presence, both physically and spiritually, whenever he or she is giving Per-sonal forming to a work. It is an empty time of life to have to sit through a singer's "reading" of a piece of music if the person does not invest something in the sound.

One Christmas Eve, a church invited various musical
ensembles to play some seasonal music for a two-hour
period of preparation for the evening service. One
of the presenters was a soloist who sang the carols
"correctly and very properly" and with degrees of
emotion and changes in volume. But, something was
lacking. Perhaps, it was because she was up in the
choir loft, in the front of the church, with the pulpit and choir railing serving as barricades. It
may have been her formal attitude, or the visible
fact that she was reading the music that seemed to
hinder the communication. Whatever it was that was
wrong, there was no personal Presence to be felt.

A Presence is a fascinating mystery that is in action,
becoming more than it was a moment ago. You sense
that creation is going on here. Transformation is
taking place. Something new and fresh is happening before us in an unrepeatable way.

Presence communicates a personal expression to be with
you, to share life with you. There is no distance between us. When we share in another's Presence, there
is growth. Presence enlarges the meaningful space in
which we can move about. We are refreshed by the
singing.

Sometimes I get the feeling that churches want the musician to be
impersonel. It's as if the musician must cut himself or herself
off from genuine feelings in order to sing God's praise. This is
certainly in contrast to the emotive style of the musician in the
scriptures in which singing, playing or dancing was done "with
all your might." You put your whole self into being God's instrument. Our fear of emoting what is inside is a sad commentary on
the condition of music in the church.

> "The public loves the same type of sterile work; the
> exploiters continue to provide it. 'Serious' com-
> posers laboriously create their arbitrary and brain-
> begotten works while the emotional element — the
> soul of art — is lost in the passion for mechanical
> perfection."

> Ernest Block
> (1880-1959)

Why do we put restrictions on being natural, feeling good or
feeling sad, when we come to church? If God knows us more deeply

than we know ourselves, why must we be so preoccupied with a formality that too often blocks honest religious expression?

We need to do away with the misinterpretation that sharing your musical skills in worship is in some way evil. If anything, the full giving of one's ability in music is to be applauded. It is a sign of God's gracious Love for His creation that he endows people with gifts and talents. Nowhere in the Bible does it tell us not to give of ourselves fully in God's service. I can't imagine God feeling displeased with a musician who pours himself out in giving per-sonal form to a work. The congregation should be filled with awe and thanksgiving that a musician of this magnitude is devoting these talents to the expression of God's Presence.

It strikes me as the height of Puritan properness when I read:

> "Singers in the Episcopal choir do not face the congregation, even during solos; their work is not to entertain, nor display musical skill. Individuality is to be effaced in singing to the glory of God and leading the congregations in the offering of their sacrifice of praise. The day will come when this will be the rule rather than the exception."
>
> from Church Facts and Principles
> by Walsh
>
> quoted in the paper "CHORAL DIRECTING AND SONG LEADING"
> by Dr. A. F. Brightbill

The problem with most of our singers in church is that they follow the directions to the letter; they neither display musical skill nor do they provide sounds that are worth listening to. We need to break away from this impersonal and pompous attitude in singing God's praise. God wants each musician to be natural. Some days that may be good. Some days that will be bad. God accepts us for all our talents and short-comings. We must learn to accept ourselves and do the very best we can whenever we are a Presence with God's People.

Dolores Layer with Rev. Kent Schneider (in background) in the 10th
Anniversary Concert of jazz in the church (January, 1976).

QUALITIES OF THE CREATIVE SINGER

<u>Sing With Natural Spirit</u>

Billy Taylor's gospel song "I Wish I Knew How It Would Feel To Be Free" is a good one for any vocalist to get into. It speaks of a need to break those chains that hold me so that I can be what I'm meant to be.

Too many singers fall short of real Spiritual heights because they are being held back by the notes on the page. We need to go beyond simply interpreting notes and begin interpreting music. I've already alluded to this distinction in the previous section on the Imitator and the Interpreter.

Dolores Layer, a member of the Center staff, is a classically-trained soprano soloist who has broadened her vocal style by getting into the traditions of the Black Gospel singer. It was a new experience for her to try singing music without paying strict attention to the note values but paying more attention to how she felt at the time when she was singing. Here's what she said:

> "At first, it was frightening to think of singing without the music. I had learned to pay specific attention to sustaining notes and holding them their full value. Now I was getting into music that invited me to free myself of the notation and sing what the music and words felt like inside.

> "It was difficult when I began. I had to do a great deal of listening to other singers in order to study what they were doing with a piece of music. I heard people 'bend' notes and 'slide' into tones, adding other notes that weren't in the melody. These were all things that were 'forbidden' to do when I was taking vocal training. The voice had to make the notes 'precisely and cleanly.'

> "Gradually, after months of listening and trying out ideas on my own, I began developing a style of my own. It is great to be able to bring my own interpretation to a piece of music and risk putting myself into it."

Father Clarence Rivers, an innovator in liturgy and music, particularly within the Catholic Church, told me that when a person is singing, he or she should sing with meaning rather than singing in a detached way. The epitome of music is communication of meaning, not the production of perfect, round tones which has become the classical thing.

> "Listen to the average, trained, classical singer," he said, "especially if you're at the opera. No matter whether you speak the language they're singing or not, you cannot understand a word they're singing, even though they are enunciating clearly.
>
> "You have the same situation in the Olympics. A skater can get into the Olympics and have great style, but make one slip and one small point is floored. Somebody else can be dull as hell, but because, technically, they did all right and didn't inspire a soul, that person got the most points.
>
> "Do you see what I mean? Overcoming this technical feeling that pervades our society will be very important. This does not mean that I want musicians to get away from technical perfection. You should give all that you can, but there is something else that is more important than technique alone. You've got to put yourself into whatever you do."

You cannot force the Spirit in singing. You must prepare yourself to be open to it.

Prepare Yourself to Sing

I know many musicians who take a few moments of quiet before they play or sing to organize themselves Spiritually. A short prayer, whether spoken out loud or within, is a helpful centering down, a time of calming, trying to touch the deepest resources inside.

A Prayer of Preparation

> Lord, open me up to Your Spirit.
> Be with me and fill me with Your music.
> Calm my anxiousness,
> Guide my spirit,
> Make me an Instrument of Your Joy.
> Lord, send me with conviction,
>   compassion and courage.
>
>   Amen

Prepare Those Who Will Hear You

If I'm in a concert setting, I will invite the people to chant with me the word "shalom." Together, we simply sing the word on one tone, but very slowly. This is a way of gathering the minds and spirits of a people together and prepares them for receiving what you are about to share.

If your music is to be a solo piece in the context of the worship movement, you will also need to prepare the people to receive your song. Too often a soloist's work feels like "the music was just stuck in" to fill up the time. You will need to prepare the listener to understand the meaning of the song, particularly if the worship service has not done so already.

> "This morning I sang 'The Child' as a solo in the worship service. It really fit in well to the whole service because all the parts, the scripture readings, the minister's words, the congregational prayers, all spoke about 'the child' that is in us, even as we grow into adulthood. The child in each of us brings joy and wonder and doesn't let life harden us. The fact that the service built around 'the child' imagery was important and made my sharing the song much easier.

> "I also had an opportunity to speak about the song before I sang it. I talked about the Epiphany season and the wise men's journey to seek the child. I spoke of the child that is in all of us and shared how the song grew out of Kent Schneider's personal experience."

> Dolores Layer, singer

Most soloists really don't take time to prepare the people for the music they are about to hear. Dolores took time to help the people to listen to some of the human drama that is in "The Child."

> "I believe that this is something that could be done more often. It could be done not only by the soloist, but also by the choir director before an anthem. I try to do this whenever I know something about the history of a song. It makes the music much more meaningful to the congregation, particularly when they have no knowledge of the music or the composer."

The Musical Selection is Integral to the Whole Service

> "I believe that it was very important that the minister's words dealt with God and His feelings for children just before I sang 'The Child.' This helped to tie my words together with the rest of the service so that there was a flow to the worship and not an abrupt stopping and starting."

It is important that all the per-sonal formers of worship work in a team spirit. This means that the minister should be aware of the music that will be sung and played and that the musicians should be aware of what the minister will be doing. In many churches, the minister knows what the choir will sing or what the soloist will sing. He may use some of the words of the song as a way of introducing the work to the congregation. This is a way of preparing the people for what they are about to hear. We must do more of this "sensitizing" in worship.

> "I believe the minister did know the song I was going to sing because the choir director and I had discussed the piece earlier. I feel that it is important for the soloist and choir director (and minister, if possible) to discuss the whole service: at what point will the solo be, how does the music fit in with the scripture and sermon? This helps the singer find greater meaning in the service.

> "That's why it is important for the minister and choir director to work together on the planning of the service. When the music ties into the whole service, there is a good flow and a focus. If possible, the soloist needs to have knowledge about the service. More and more, churches are finding the importance of the minister and the musician working together on designing worship. I believe that there are soloists who are interested, too."

Movement in the Sanctuary

How can the soloist become more than just "someone up there" in the choir loft? Are there ways that you can enable the congregation to understand that you are offering your singing as a part of the life of the community?

> "One of the traditional things with a soloist in church has been standing in the choir loft because that's where people expect to 'see' you. I've recently tried moving among the congregation when I sing a solo. By moving among the people and looking at their faces, I'm able to sense more about them and feel that my communication is much closer with them.

> "Singing from behind the people is challenging, too. I try harder to get the music across. This is especially effective as a call to worship — a solo voice coming from the balcony really lets the words 'float' over the people."

It is too easy to get locked into the architecture of the church. People come to expect the minister in "his place" and the choir in "their place." But, if the church and all its ministers (the congregation) is to be at work throughout the everyday world, then there is no such thing as having "my place." We need to develop the sense of mobility and flexibility within the space we use for worship.

"Today was the first experience I had moving with the microphone when I sang. I moved up one aisle and then the other one, crossing over in front of the altar area. I really felt that the people were with me because I was there among them, not standing somewhere 'up there.' In fact, I would have liked to have taken off my choir robe, but the director wanted me to keep it on. There's something about wearing a choir robe that throws me back into a church where the musicians are set apart from the congregation. I feel it is essential for the musicians to be seen as part of the congregation. I could have felt even more a part of the congregation if I had been dressed as they were.

"Sometimes I feel that the choir's dress is a block to people feeling the music, particularly newer music."

Feel the Freedom of the Music

Most soloists use music when they sing. I feel that the solo singer has a unique opportunity to be free of the notes and to interpret the words in a freer style than a choir would be.

"It was a good feeling not to use music. I could put everything of myself into the song without having to worry about what notes or words were coming up next. I could look at the people and sense their feelings. I'm much more into what's happening when I don't use the music. It's important that the music be done well, but being expressive of the words and feeling that are in the work is also important. When you don't have to worry about the music, then all your energy can be directed to getting the music across.

"Our exposure to the best singers through television and in films has made the public aware of how personal the communication can be when music is not used or music stands aren't needed. Our congregation may be expecting this same kind of professionalism from the soloist."

VOCAL SOLO COLLECTIONS

Songs of Love by Kent Schneider

    The Child
    Songs Of Love
    Greet The Dawn
    Burst Of Christ
    Bread of Presence
    Mary's Song
    Nothin' Left To Fear
    Life Is A Circle

The Center for Contemporary
   Celebration
West Lafayette, IN Publ.

(Variety of music for the
  liturgical year.)

Come Share the Spirit by Kent Schneider

    Many songs adaptable for solo work.

The Center for Contemporary
   Celebration
West Lafayette, IN Publ.

The Alfred Burt Carols   Words by Alfred Burt
                 Arranged by Wilha
                  Hutson

    Sets I-II-III-IV

Shawnee Press Inc.
Delaware Water Gap, PA

(Arranged for choir, but can
  be used as solos.)

Die Weihnachlsgeschichte   Arranged by Carl Orff

    # 3 Dormi Jesu
    # 9 Amor Amor
    #26 O My deir Hert
    #28 Mater et filia
    #31 Mary at the Cross
    #32 A Good-night

Available through Indiana
   University Music Library
Bloomington, IN

(Collection of early church
  songs, suitable for Lent
  and Advent, with instrumental background.)

Afro-American Spirituals, Work Songs and Ballads

                    Edited by Alan Lomax

From the Archives of American Folk Songs
Library of Congress
           AAFS L3

Afro-American Blues and Game Songs

                    Edited by Alan Lomax

From the Archives of American Folk Songs
Library of Congress
           A-FS-L4

Sacred Songs from Schemelli's Gesangbuch

          by J.S. Bach

Concordia Publishing House
St. Louis, MO

Cantata and Oratorio Selections

Pie Jesu   from "Requiem" by Gabriel Fauré   Fitzsimons Publ. Co.

I Know That My Redeemer Liveth   from "Messiah" by   G. Schirmer Publ. Co.
                                    G. F. Handel

Come Unto Him   from "Messiah" by   G. Schirmer Publ. Co.
                                    G. F. Handel

Ah My Savior from "Christmas Oratorio" by J. S. Bach   G. Schirmer Publ. Co.

If With All Your Hearts from "Elijah" by F. Mendelssohn G. Schirmer Publ. Co.

Sheet Music

Gospel and Folk

God Has Smiled On Me

A Clean Heart

Give Me A Clean Heart

God Is So Good To Me

I'm Glad

Joy Like A River

I Wish I Knew How It Would Feel To Be Free   by Billy Taylor

I Wonder As I Wander   Arranged by John Jacob Niles   G. Schirmer Publ. Co.

The Lone Wild Bird   Arranged by David Johnson   Augsburg Publ. Co.

Ah Jesus Lord, Thy Love To Me   Arranged by David   Augsburg Publ. Co.
                                   Johnson

Jesus, Jesus, Rest Your Head   Traditional American   R. D. Row Publ. Co.
                                                          (John Edmunds, ed.)
                                                          Boston, MA

Turning Point by Martha Holmes

Come Sunday from "Black, Brown and Beige" by Duke Ellington

Bless This House   Music by May H. Brahe   Boosey & Hawkes
                    Words by Helen Taylor

His Eye Is On The Sparrow   Traditional

Bless This House by Blanche Ebert Seaver   Sam Fox Publ. Co.

Bless The Lord, O My Soul by Clement W. Barker   R. D. Row Music Co.
                                                     Boston, MA

The Lord Is My Shepherd by Samuel Liddle   Boosey & Co. Ltd.
      Psalm XXXIII

The Ward-Stephans Musical Setting of Poems   by Anne   G. Schirmer Publ. Co.
      based on "The Beatitudes"   Campbell
                                                     (Solo for each of the
                                                      Beatitudes.)

The Virgins Slumber Song by Max Reger   Associated Publ. Co.

Prayer by David W. Guion   G. Schirmer Publ. Co.

How Lovely Are Thy Dwellings by Samuel Liddle   Boosey & Hawkes

Oh Divine Redeemer by Charles Gounod   Carl Fischer Inc.
      Repentier   Parce Domine

At The Cry Of The First Bird by David W. Guion   G. Schirmer Publ. Co.

Prayer-Lord God Almighty from "The Moscow Cantata" Galaxy Music Corp.
                          by P. I. Tchaikovsky   New York

Oh Lord Most Holy (Panis Angelicus) by Cesar Franck The Boston Music Co.

Whither Shall I Go From Thy Spirit by James G. MacDermid Forester Music Publ.
                                                     Chicago, IL

The Frostbound Wood by Peter Warlock   Oxford Publ.

My Soul Doth Magnify The Lord by Randall Thompson   E. C. Schirmer

THE WELL-TEMPERED CHOIR...
and ITS DIRECTOR

The style and function of choral music is changing. No longer is
it enough for the local choir to simply present an anthem and
sing the seven-fold "Amen." Choral directors and clergy are realizing the sound possibilities for church musicians and the flexibility that will be necessary for choirs to more fully share in
worship.

Versatility is going to be a guiding light for the future of
choirs. The ability to sing a wide range of musical styles will
be essential. A basic repertoire of responses, chants and anthems
should be committed to memory. This will be important so that,
when the mood of the celebration changes, the choir will be able
to "spontaneously" move with the flow.

> I have attended many worship services in which
> the choir's anthem seemed to be the most con-
> spicuously inappropriate part of the service.
> The feeling in the service was one of joy and
> uplifting hope and then the choir comes on with
> some drag of a piece that plunges the momentum
> into the grave. Such deadliness is a disaster.

The choir will need to function like a good-working band in which
certain tunes are "head charts" — the musicians know the music
well enough that the director need only to tell the people what
they are going to sing and to tell the organist what key they
will do it in, and the song happens. That's the kind of choir
that is responsive to the needs of the community. That's the
kind of church musicians that can serve the people, instead of
simply singing at the congregation.

The potential of every choir is to be a Spirit-voice of the people.
In order to do this, the director will need to expand his or her
musical knowledge to include various styles of musical expression:
folk, jazz, rock, electronics, polyphonic, chants, in addition to
the classic literature of the church. Choirs need to push themselves to expand their versatility by developing small units
within the choir.

It is now time to get beyond the 19th-century concept of a choir
whose sole role is to sing the time-honored anthems from robed
lofts. The choir is a musical extension of the whole community
and the choir director is a minister with particular responsibilities and gifts.

The Creative Director

The following is an interview with Bob Ray, professor of music at the University of Illinois, Champaign-Urbana, and the director at his local church. This conversation took place during August, 1975. Bob was serving as a resource leader at the Afro-American Conference on Liturgy and Music at St. Joseph's College in Indiana:

Kent: What is the role of the choir director in worship?

Bob: It's probably two-fold: first, you are to train and prepare the musical members of the choir for the actual worship; secondly, the choir director ends up being a kind of minister of music, that is, he's responsible for all the music-making in the church and he plans the total spectrum of music for the entire year.

In the Black Church, the choir director selects the hymns that we are going to sing that morning. Contrary to popular belief, we still do sing hymns in the Black Church. We sing some straight old "Holy, Holy, Holy's" and "A Mighty Fortress Is Our God."

Kent: What is the role of the choir in the Black Church?

Bob: The choir serves as a spiritually motivating force. It's one of several institutions in the church. Other than the preacher, it's probably the single, largest, most important tradition in the Black Church. The choral tradition is rapidly being established now. Before, the whole congregation was the choir. Now, we have trained choirs that sing in the services, but there is still that healthy mixture of the old style where everybody sings together with the choir.

Kent: What should church musicians listen to in order to get a good feel for contemporary gospel music?

Bob: You need to go back and listen to some old gospel music first. I'd recommend James Cleveland as representative of the old school. Look for his initial album with the James Cleveland Singers. They represent the foundations, especially in choral singing, because gospel singing was not a choral tradition for a long time. It was primarily solos and quartets. It's only been in the last 15-20 years

that the choral tradition of very large mass choirs
has come into existence. Thomas A. Dorsey, probably
one of the pioneers of gospel movement (still living
in Chicago), wrote hundreds of solo songs that have now
been turned into choral arrangements. There's an album
of Dorsey's work, a collection of his greatest hits
("Peace In The Valley," "Precious Lord Take My Hand,"
 "I'll Tell It Wherever I Go") that is available.

Then in the contemporary scene, you have Edwin Hawkins,
Andre Crouch and Beverly Glenn (who is in Detroit).

Kent: Are the recordings the way that the oral tradition is
        carried on?

Bob: I think so, but, with the generations coming up, they
        are getting more into the reading of music. Maybe,
        in another 20 years, the printed page will become more
        important than listening to the sound. But, for
        right now, the records are part of the oral tradition.
        A person chooses a particular song primarily because
        he heard it somewhere. He'll just take the song off
        the album and teach it to the choir. I went to a
        couple of workshops with James Cleveland and I just
        made sure that I held the song he taught us in my
        mind long enough to get home to a piano and work it
        out on the keyboard. So, it's pretty much an oral
        tradition.

Kent: What is the difference when a group sings from an
        oral tradition or when a group sings from a reading
        tradition (music from a printed page)?

Bob: The word I think of is "inhibition" when you're read-
        ing. You get so involved with the visual (the re-
        lationship of a note to a rest, or middle "C" to "G",
        or this phrase goes up and this one goes down), you
        get so involved with the mechanics of music-making
        that you completely miss the spirit behind the music.
        I prefer not to have the words in front of my singers.
        I want them to absorb the meaning through hearing it.
        The problem with reading is that it keeps you from
        being as free as you could be. Once you've learned
        the notes, then you have to go back and get into the
        spiritual things you want to come out of the music.
        I find it better if the people catch the spirit of the
        music by hearing it from me and then we can go back
        over it and work on the fine points of expression. It
        is through the oral tradition that you keep that spirit
        alive.

Kent: Your choirs clap when they sing. Is that something
        that you rehearse or is that totally spontaneous?

Bob: The only reason you would rehearse clapping is if the
        rhythm patterns are difficult in a song. There are
        some songs that are so fast that the singers have dif-
        ficulty keeping the steadiness of the beat. The holi-
        ness churches use clapping a lot. The Baptists, not
        quite as much. The Methodists, well.....clapping
        seems almost impossible. And, for Catholics, Lutherans
        and Episcopalians, you might as well forget it. Clap-
        ping adds a dynamic intensity to a song. In the Black
        Church, the choir sings with big voices and the voices
        can be heard over the clapping. But, with the Catholics,
        they've encouraged well-trained, beautiful, little
        voices. If you clap too loud, you can't hear the voices.

Kent: A lot of churches sing half-heartedly and the choir's
        music is kind of mediocre, there's no life or rhythm
        to the music. Some people are afraid of music that has
        rhythm. I'd be interested in knowing your views.

Bob: Don't isolate the concept of rhythm from the concept of
        culture. The whole Afro-American culture makes the
        beat mandatory. Coming out of Africa, with the extreme
        rhythmic-ness of the people, and transplanting that
        whole cultural tradition on American soil, it dictates
        that you've got to keep the rhythmic intensity going.
        It's part of the life-style and influences what goes
        on in the Black Church. Because of the segregation,
        there was little opportunity for black churches and
        white churches to get together. Now, there is that
        opportunity for over-lapping. White Americans are
        sensing that maybe there is a blend happening in the
        church. Maybe there is an over-staidness in the wor-
        ship structure and, perhaps, they need some more
        spontaneous things in worship.

Kent: I sense a real hunger among a generation of young adults,
        who have matured with the popular music of their day
        which has its roots in the rhythm and blues music of
        the black musician, for a style of church music that
        expresses their feelings. How do you introduce con-
        temporary music in worship?

Bob: Even in the most puritanical and conservative churches,
        people are finally recognizing contemporary sounds in
        music. An easy way would be to take some of the real
        contemporary gospel music that the people could relate

to. Don't go in there bumping, jumping and stomping
with old-style gospel. Take some mild-mannered Edwin
Hawkins music and gradually work the choir into a more
progressive program. Don't go in trying to upset an
apple cart, because all you will be doing is alienating
a lot of people. Maybe, when you play hymns, instead
of playing them straight, find an organist who can add
little touches of improvisation or put a gentle, little
beat behind it.

Kent: How does the organist or pianist develop in the Black
        Church?

Bob: It's primarily an oral tradition, too. It's one in
        which you just sit down and, through trial and error,
        just learn to play. Nobody teaches you to play gospel.

        Traditionally, when the preacher "tunes up," the
        instruments get behind him and play. I really felt
        sorry for my preacher the first couple of times I had
        to "tune up" with him. It was horrible, attrocious.
        I didn't know what I was doing. I couldn't find his
        note or the chords.

        A lot of times a preacher will light out into a song.
        If he takes off in the key of B Major, then you've
        got to catch him in that key. You've got to be able
        to play all the chords in B just as easily as you do
        in D or A^b. So, it's a matter of trial and error and
        getting a chance to play as much as you can. Soon, it's
        a part of your life-style.

Kent: How would an organist develop this style, if he'd
        never played it before?

Bob: The best way is to go to a Black Church and listen and
        observe. You've just got to feel it. There are a lot
        of little churches that are in need of musicians. Here
        is an opportunity for someone who doesn't have the ex-
        perience to go and say: "Here I am. I'm willing to
        work and learn, if you're willing to put up with me and
        help me learn!" I think that would be the easiest way
        to get involved.

Kent: How did you work with your minister in preparing for
        worship?

Bob: We work well together. It's built on mutual respect:
        "Okay, you're the musician. I will give you the ball
        and you run with it. If you get it all flubbed up,

I'm going to come in and we're going to have some counseling sessions." But, as long as things are going well, he doesn't interfere with the choir work. It's a very healthy situation. We don't interfere with his preaching work. We don't step on his toes and he doesn't step on ours. It's really incredible, because the relationship between the choir director and the preacher has always been strained in the Black Church. But, we get along well.

I was really impressed with the sense of ministry which Bob brought to his choral work. Not only was he a highly versatile player, skilled in classics as well as the gospel tradition, but he was also a committed person of faith. His choir was a spiritual time. He took time to pray with the choir or he invited someone in the choir to pray. He was a very contagious leader. "At least I know what I should be doing," said Bob, "and I want other people to have that same joy, the same kind of joy that I found in Jesus Christ. And, so, that's my ministry. I do it through music. Ministers do it through the priests' work."

Further Reading

BLACK AMERICAN MUSIC: PAST AND PRESENT, Hildred Roach. Boston: Crescendo Publishing Company, 1973.

BLACK MUSIC IN AMERICA, John Rublowsky. New York: Basic Books, 1971.

THE MUSIC OF BLACK AMERICANS: A HISTORY, Eileen Southern. New York: W. W. Norton, 1971.

THE SPIRITUAL AND THE BLUES, James H. Cone. New York: Seabury Press, 1972.

VOCAL IMPROVISATION METHOD, Bert Konowitz. New York: Alfred Music Co., Inc.

HAND-CLAPPING

<u>Expressive Communication</u>

> "I feel the crowd with me when I get that first hand as
> I get up on the stand, then it's up to me to play.
> The public's ready to give you a hand for anything
> you play good. Whatever you do play — play it good."

> Louis Armstrong
> from <u>THE LOUIS ARMSTRONG STORY</u>, pages 219-220

Applause is a natural expression of appreciation and thanksgiving. It is another way of praying that gives thanks for the creative Presence of God within a musician.

It is obvious that we don't use the expressive medium of clapping in church enough. I've been a part of many worship services in which hand-clapping, either in time with the music or as a sound of appreciation for what's been heard, would have been the most natural response. After the service, people would say, "I wanted to clap, but I wasn't sure if it would be alright, being that we're in church, you know." Not only must the creative musician free himself or herself up, but we also have a ministry to speak a word of freedom to the congregations. Underneath a century of repressed feelings, there are people in your congregation who are waiting for an invitation to be natural when the church gathers.

> "Clap your hands, all peoples!
>   Shout to God with loud songs of joy!"

> Psalm 47

You may have to invite the congregation to express itself in appreciating the music.

> When I'm playing religious jazz somewhere as a part of
> a worship event, I explain to the people that the
> musicians come with a purpose in their playing. They
> are not here to dazzle you with their technique. They
> are here to give thanks to God and to witness to God's
> Presence in their own lives. The musician will be say-
> ing things through his horn, much like the minister
> uses words. We believe that God can work through all
> instruments of creation, through all kinds of people.
> If you feel that it's a natural expression for you to

clap, do so. You are clapping for God's Presence that is in each and every person. It is good to use your whole body in the worship of the Lord.

Listening to music is not a passive role. Without the listener, there can be no music. There needs to be ways of participating and responding to the music. Again, I go back to the idea of worship being a call and response. The music is like a call that goes out to the congregation to gather for worship and prepare for the Spirit. The congregation can respond in many ways to the call: in sung hymns, spoken and silent prayers, with an "amen" and with applause.

Clapping and Rhythm Accompaniment

Contemporary church music is much more rhythmic than the church music of a century ago. When we sing these new songs, we often need to provide a stronger rhythmic accompaniment than just the guitar or the piano.

What can a congregation do when they don't have maracas, claves or tambourines? They can use their hands!

Hands are great, natural rhythm instruments. Small children know that. They clap out rhythms as a part of their learning in school. Clapping helps our coordination.

In the Georgia Sea Islands, the choirs not only sing, but they clap and stomp. They use their whole bodies in the service of God. They voice the clapping sounds:

> the bass clap: made with very hollow, cupped hands, giving a deep sound;
>
> the tenor clap: made with the flat palms, giving a slapping, middle-range sound; and
>
> the soprano clap: made by clapping on the fingers, giving a softer sound.

In orchestrating a choir for clapping, you'll need more soprano clappers than tenors and more tenors than bass. This is simply because of the difference in volume of each kind of clap.

On the following page, there are several clapping patterns that you can begin with.

PATTERN NUMBER 1   Waltz

PATTERN NUMBER 2   March

PATTERN NUMBER 3   Bossa Nova

These should be taught by rote, not by reading. Teach the bass part
first, then add the tenor, then the soprano.

Let your choir use these as warm-up rhythm exercises. Once they've
got the feel of the simpler patterns, invite them to suggest other
patterns so that they develop their sense of timing and improvisation.

<u>Clapping and Singing</u>

> "When people clap to music, that's a cop-out. The
> real thing is to get them singing. Singing and
> clapping, that's alright, but just clapping, that's
> too easy."
>
> Theo Bikel, actor, composer, musician

Now that your people have gotten into clapping, let's add the singing.

Using Pattern number 1 (the 3/4 pattern), and again, teaching the
bass clap first, then the tenor, try singing the hymn "Praise Ye
The Lord." Have half of the choir or congregation hold the hymnals
while the other half does the clapping.

> We were with Reverend Norm Brinkman, in New Jersey,
> at worship one Sunday morning. He had an acoustic
> guitarist and a pianist for the accompaniment of
> the hymns. The congregation numbered nearly 400
> people. One of the hymns was "Praise Ye The Lord."
> I wanted the congregation to feel some of the drive
> and power of that hymn, but, with only the two in-
> struments, it would be very difficult to drive the
> singing. I explained to the community that this
> song of praise needed their power and rhythm. I
> invited half of the congregation to clap (the bass
> clap on the first beat of the measure) and the
> other half to sing. The result was a tremendous
> singing experience.

You might try using Pattern number 1 with the hymn "Now Thank
We All Our God" (in a 3/4 meter).

The hymn "All You People, Clap Your Hands," by Ray Repp, would be
another simple way of introducing clapping to the congregation.

My hymn "The Church Within Us" is to be sung in a bossa nova style,
for which you could try adding Pattern number 3. "They'll Know We
Are Christians By Our Love" is also a bossa nova.

Two things are important:

> first, don't just try this once with your choir or
> congregation as a novelty. Keep introducing clapping
> and singing ideas so that people become more familiar
> with the rhythmic involvement of their whole bodies
> when they sing; and secondly, not every hymn is in
> need of clapping. Select out those texts that refer

to an imagery of clapping (Psalm 47:1; 98:8). Begin
with these, since the act of clapping is obvious.

♩hoir ♪ot♯s

I have found that where a choir sits, stands or moves is a subtle communication as to the style of celebration. To continually place a choir in a loft or in pews, week after week, may be impressive but not always imaginative.

Encourage the choir to experiment with its sound: singing from within the congregation, singing while surrounding the congregation, singing antiphonally from one side to the other or from the front to the back.

Another interesting sound experience is to arrange the choir vertically instead of horizontally. This can be accomplished by arranging the choir on a stairwell, or by having part of the choir in a balcony while the other part is directly below them. We need to explore the sound possibilites beyond just the horizontal.

The director should also consider his or her place in the liturgy. I feel that congregational members could appreciate the music of the choir more if they were not watching the movements of the director. I remember, as a teenager, watching the energetic directings of the choir leader. I didn't listen to the music, I watched the director. Now that I'm a bit older, I enjoy hearing the music. I think choir directors should minimize their visual gestures for most of the material sung by a choir. The director is to coordinate and interpret the music. If this can be done in rehearsal, Sunday-morning choirs might start using their ears instead of their eyes — which could improve the quality of choirs.

SOUND EXPLORATIONS FOR THE CHOIR

The choir as greeters.

Consider the experience of coming into church and being greeted by members of your choir while other members are singing. Or the possibility of the choir greeting the people by singing an anthem outside the church building and, then, enter singing. Let the choir also greet the people at the end of the service.

Call to worship.	In a recent service, the congregation processed into the sanctuary singing "Come Ye Thankful People, Come." As the community arrived, a small choir encircled the altar table (which was situated in the round).
	The liturgist spoke: "It is a good thing to give thanks to the Lord and to sing praises to His name." Immediately, the choir began to sing a Bach chorale (a capella) which picked up the theme of singing praise. The congregation then joined in a communal prayer.
	Another simple format which blends liturgist, community and choir is the following:
A Litany format with choir.	Liturgist: At your invitation, Father, we gather as one family. People: We come in trust and confidence that Your Presence sustains us. (Choir response is sung. Perhaps simply an "Alleluia" as in "Christ the Lord Is Risen Today.") Liturgist: Your Love surrounds us. People: Your Spirit grows within us. (Choir response.) Liturgist: Bring us to a fullness of energy. People: That we might act with justice, compassion and joyous thanksgiving for all that we have been given. (Choir response.)
	The liturgist regulates the speed of movement, waiting for the choir to sing their response and then speaking the next line. The words "choir response" would not be printed in the bulletin since the liturgist would know of their entrance.
Sounding the Scriptures.	The Bible is filled with sound images. Consider Psalm 150 ("Praise him with the trumpet") or Psalm 98 ("Sing a new song to the Lord"). In addition to reading the words, let sound make the words become events. For example, Psalm 150 could be read to the improvised accompaniment of trumpet, stringed instruments, tambourine and

cymbal. Psalm 98 could include teaching a simple song to the congregation which could be sung while the Psalm was being read. Solo instruments (cello, flute, french horn) can effectively translate the meaning of scripture. Sound can create the environment in which scripture can be read. A choral arrangement of Psalm 98 is available from The Center for SATB choir with combinations of flute, saxes, trumpet, trombone, piano, bass or drums.

Prayer and Sound.

"OM" is a sound prayer-chant, meaning "all life is God" or "All life is good." It is droned on a note that each person can comfortably reach. When a group does this prayer-chant, it has the calming effect of a pipe organ playing softly.

Another thought: let the anthem serve as a prayer on behalf of the community. The liturgist might say: "Let us pray." And, the choir would begin.

A meaningful blending of music and prayer at the Offertory was developed at St. Thomas the Apostle Church in Chicago. The liturgist says: "Let us pray for the needs of those around us." The choir responds with: "Lord, hear our prayer." On the word "prayer," the choir sustains the note, humming. The liturgist continues while the choir sustains the note. After each petition, the choir raises the sung response one full step.

The Choral Offering.

At certain times, it may be very appropriate that members of the choir would receive the offering. Offerings are more than "bread", they are our creativity and our ability. As part of an offering, the choir might make a vocal gift. Encourage members to create original music for such an occasion.

INTRODUCING NEW MUSIC
TO THE CONGREGATION

The role of the musician in worship is much like that of the minister: to enable, to encourage, to cajole, to illustrate, to be honest and to share life and love together. The musician can take various styles in being a part of worship. Two styles are:

as <u>performer</u> where you add your own <u>per</u>-sonal <u>form</u> to an idea

OR

as <u>enabler</u> where you take on a transparent quality in order to help others give form to their feelings and ideas.

I personally feel that the style of <u>enabler</u> is often more useful than that of performer. Enabler embodies a style of invitation... to "come and share." The performer is characterized by a style of witnessing... a testimony. Both styles are useful. We must develop a sensitivity to know when they are appropriate.

Preparation of the Music

It is very important that you select or compose songs which build the flow of the service. The music should add to the meaning of the content, rather than take away from that meaning.

In selecting congregational music for worship, consider the following points:

- <u>Read the text for its meaning.</u>

  Determine what it is saying. What kind of imagery is used? How many verses are appropriate? How can the singing of this hymn become an event?

- <u>At what tempo should the song be sung?</u>

  Remember, speed kills, but traveling too slowly is also deadly.

- <u>What rhythmic accompaniments are appropriate for the song?</u>

  I have a hunch that not every verse of the hymn should be sung or played the same way. If a verse expresses something different than the preceding verse, shouldn't the accompaniment also sound different than before?

- <u>What melodic accompaniments are appropriate for the song?</u>

  If you are near a high school or college which has a band program, you probably have the opportunity of unlimited instrumental accompaniments. Let your imagination roll.

- Check the key of the song.

  The right song in the wrong key is a disaster. Check the range of the song for your congregation's voice. You may want to modulate (change keys) for certain verses to build the intensity and drama.

- Help the musicians who will be part of the service to understand how they fit into the whole event.

  You may want to explain to the musicians that they are ministering to the congregation through their instruments. Take time to pray together so that they feel more a part of the whole musical ministry of your people.

- When you're introducing a new song, either with words or with the music itself, do it with conviction and spirit.

  Nothing is more threatening to a congregation than a musician explaining: "Well, this is a new song we've really just started working on. We don't have it too much together yet, but we hope you will want to sing along with us." Help your musicians understand that they are the music that they make. If the musical leading is weak and timid, the people will sing it that way.

  My experience has been that people want to cooperate with someone who believes in what he or she is doing. Your attitude will convey a lot about how much the congregation should participate in the music.

  Project the spirit of the song. Let there be life in the tune.

- Clear enunciation is important.

  People naturally respond better when they can understand what is being said or sung.

- Introduce the song with an invitation rather than a command.

  Nothing is more deadening than someone getting up and saying: "We will now sing hymn number 234!" That is a command and very impersonal. A better method could be by inviting the people with a phrase: "Would you join with the community in singing the hymn 'God of Our Fathers'?" or "Let's rise in singing 'Christ The Lord Is Risen Today'."

  You can also tie your introduction of the hymn into the service by quoting some of the words of the hymn. For example,

"As we come to a time of communion, let us prepare ourselves to break bread together."

Then, don't just begin the song and have the organist play it one time through. The organist could be giving the intro-duction while the words of invitation are being said so that, when the words are finished, all can begin singing. Inter-weave the music into the service.

- Avoid a "hymn-sandwich" service.

You can't put new wine into old wineskins. The same goes with the new music. Don't expect the music to be able to simply fit into the old slots. You will have to think through the whole service with the people planning it and interweave the music. Don't be satisfied with that old hymn-sandwich. It's years old and has gone stale.

- Keep a record of what hymns are sung and when.

This will keep you from settling on a few old favorites week after week. Periodically, tape the music for the purpose of evaluating your style of introduction and the quality of the music.

THE SPIRIT OF SINGING

What Is A Hymn?

It is a song with praise of God.

If you praise God, but don't sing, you utter no hymn.
If you sing, but praise not God, you utter no hymn.
A hymn contains these two things: song (canticum) and praise (laudem) of God. Praise of God in a song, then, is called a hymn.

paraphrased from Augustine

Why Do We Sing Hymns?

Our song on earth is speech. It is the sung Word. Why do Christians sing when they are together? The reason is because in singing together, it is possible for them to speak and pray the same Word at the same time, because they can unite in the Word. The fact that we do not speak it, but sing it only, expresses the fact that our spoken words are inadequate to express what we want to say, that the burden of our song goes far beyond all human words.

Dietrich Bonhoeffer
from Life Together, page 59

In singing, we learn the faith and give witness to and confess our faith together.

> We must endeavor to understand as fully as possible what we are doing when we rise to sing. We do not sing to "stretch our legs," to have a welcome change of activity, or to fill the gaps between other parts of the service. Nor do we sing to help or cheer ourselves, or to induce the right mood of listening to the sermon.

from <u>The Baptist Hymn Book Companion,</u> page 29

> A hymn combines Christ's truth with our own experiences as we are influenced by the Scriptures.

<u>How Shall We Sing?</u>

Sing All: as frequently as you can; if it be a cross to you, take it up and you will find it a blessing;

Sing lustily: and with a good courage;

Sing modestly: do not bawl, but strive to unite your voices together, so as to make one clear harmonious sound;

Sing in time: whatever tune is sung, be sure to keep with it;

Sing spiritually: have an eye to God in every word you sing; aim at pleasing Him more than yourself.

John Wesley

LITURGICAL RESOURCE ORGANIZATIONS

* * *

The Center For Contemporary Celebration
P. O. Box 3024
West Lafayette, Indiana 47906

Ecumenical resources
for jazz, folk, rock
and choral groups.

Center For Worship Reformation
P.O. Box 1052
Albany, Oregon 97321

Ecumenical resources
for worship design.

Folk Liturgies Unlimited
48 South 14th Street
Pittsburgh, Pennsylvania 15203

Ecumenical resources
for folk materials.

Folk Mass and Modern Liturgy
Resource Publications
6244 Rainbow Drive
San Jose, California 95129

An excellent resource
magazine for music and
liturgy.

Friends of the English Liturgy
1543 West Olympic Boulevard
Los Angeles, California 90075

Catholic folk mass
resources.

Hope Publishing Company
Carol Stream, Illinois 60187

Publishers of popular
folk hymnals.

North American Liturgy Resources
300 East McMillian Street
Cincinnati, Ohio 45219

Catholic folk mass
resources.

Proclamation Productions
7 Kingston Avenue
Port Jervis, New York 12271

Hymn and choral re-
sources.

Vangard Music Records
250 West 75th Street
New York, New York 10019

Ecumenical resources for
folk, choral and
instrumental groups.

World Library of Sacred Music
2145 Central Parkway
Cincinnati, Ohio 45214

Publishers of choral
and instrumental re-
sources.

Index of Names

N

North American Liturgy Resources 199

O

O'Connor, Jr., Rev. Norman J. 44,55
Ortegel, Sr. Adelaide, S.P. 63,112
Ortmayer, Rev. Roger 37
Owens, Rev. Robert 57

P

Parker, Charlie 3
Pike, Bishop James A. 93
Pope Paul 44,47
Proclamation Productions 199

R

Ray, Bob 182-186
Repp, Ray 52,190
Rivers, Rev. Clarence J. 51,174
Rotary Connection 59

S

Sanders, Pharoah 25
Santana, Carlos 61
Schaeffer, Murray 8
Schifrin, Lalo 55-56
Scholtes, Pete 52-53, 97
Shaw, Gene 29-30
Snyder, Dr. Ross 37-40
Stiffler, Rev. Paul E. 34,56,62,158-167
Sullivan, Ira 3,17-18,57
Summerlin, Ed 37,40-41, 42,56, 59-60

V

Vanguard Music Records 199

W

Werle, Floyd 139-140
Wesley, John 36,49,198
Weston, Randy 55
Williams, Mary Lou 43,56
Winter, Sr. Mariam Therese 53
Wintergate, Kathy 110
World Library of Sacred Music 199

Y

Ylvisaker, John 52

Topical Index